How to Use Technology Effectively in Post-Compulsory Education

The use of technology within the lifelong learning sector brings many benefits to learners, teachers and managers. Aimed at trainee and practising teachers, this book contains clear, practical guidance on how to use technology and e-learning effectively to enhance all aspects of teaching and learning in the post-compulsory sector.

Alan Clarke explains the technologies that are available and how to use them, from whiteboards and virtual learning environments to digital photographs, podcasts and e-portfolios. Each chapter is fully aligned with the new LLUK standards and includes teaching strategies, practical examples and case studies to show how these work in practice.

Chapters include guidance on:

- Using e-portfolios, blogs and wikis to present and share information with colleagues and encourage reflection
- Motivating students and promoting collaboration using mobile devices, discussion groups and forums
- How to use ICT to develop literacy and numeracy skills
- Ways to keep up to date with new and emerging technologies
- Using technology safely and securely.

Including a wide range of activities, questions for reflective practice and links to further sources of information, this essential textbook will help trainee and practising teachers in post-compulsory education to understand the major Information and Learning Technology (ILT) tools and use them confidently and effectively in their teaching.

Alan Clarke was Associate Director for ICT and Learning at the National Institute of Adult Continuing Education for 13 years.

How to Use Technology Effectively in Post-Compulsory Education

Alan Clarke

Routledge
Taylor & Francis Group

LONDON AND NEW YORK

First published 2011
by Routledge
2 Park Square, Milton Park, Abingdon, Oxon OX14 4RN

Simultaneously published in the USA and Canada
by Routledge
711 Third Avenue, New York, NY 10017

Routledge is an imprint of the Taylor & Francis Group, an informa business

British Library Cataloguing in Publication Data
A catalogue record for this book is available from the British Library

Library of Congress Cataloging in Publication Data
Clarke, Alan, 1952–
    How to use technology effectively in post-compulsory education / Alan Clarke.
    p. cm.
    Includes index.
    1. Continuing education—Great Britain—Computer-assisted instruction.
    2. Digital communications—Study and teaching (Continuing education)—Great Britain.
    3. Information technology—Study and teaching (Continuing education)—Great Britain.
    4. Adult education—Great Britain—Computer-assisted instruction. 5. Post-compulsory
    education—Great Britain—Computer-assisted instruction. 6. Educational technology—
    Great Britain. 7. Teaching—Great Britain—Aids and devices. I. Title.
    LC5225.D38C53 2011
    374'.260941—dc22
    2010053016

ISBN: 978–0–415–59132–4 (hbk)
ISBN: 978–0–415–59133–1 (pbk)
ISBN: 978–0–203–81741–4 (ebk)

Typeset in Bembo
by Swales & Willis Ltd, Exeter, Devon

Printed and bound in Great Britain by
TJ International Ltd, Padstow, Cornwall

To Harry, our first grandchild, who arrived while I was
writing this book.

Contents

Illustrations

Figures

Tables

Acknowledgements

The author and publisher would like to thank:

LLUK for permission to use their teaching standards

Xtensis for their permission to include a screen capture of the NLN materials website home page

Wordle (http://www.wordle.net/) for the use of their tool to create a Wordle image

Elluminate for their permission to use and supplying a screen image

Mahara for their permission to include a screen capture of their website

Microsoft and Google for permission to reproduce screenshots of their applications

Introduction

Introduction

The book is aimed at those who are experienced, newly qualified or studying to become teachers who want to learn how to employ technology in their teaching. It provides a practical insight into how teachers can employ technology to best effect. There are many practical examples of how e-learning can assist in the wide range of contexts that exist in the lifelong learning sector. Each chapter will in turn discuss technology and e-learning, with an emphasis on providing examples and case studies that teachers could employ in their work. The book has comprehensive links to further sources of information and opportunities to reflect on how to develop your confidence, skills and understanding.

Lifelong Learning United Kingdom (LLUK) is the sector skills council responsible for staff working in the post-compulsory sector. This includes further education, adult and community learning and work-based learning. In these areas staff are often called by a variety of names such as teacher, trainer and instructor. This book is aimed at anyone who works in the sector supporting learners. I have used the term teacher throughout the book to encompass all the different titles. LLUK has developed professional standards for staff working in lifelong learning (LLUK, 2007). In addition LLUK has considered the role that technology plays in learning and produced guides and reviews to assist you. These are available from the council's website. The book is intended to cover the requirements of the professional standards to assist new teachers studying to become qualified teachers. The start of each chapter indicates the coverage of the material with regard to the standards.

Activity 1.1 Technology standards

Visit the LLUK website (http://www.lluk.org/) and identify what assistance they offer teachers with regard to technology enhanced learning. You should be able to locate standards, guides and links to blogs and twitter. How would you judge yourself against the technology elements in the standards?

What is e-learning?

The application of technology to learning has had a variety of names. Currently the main terms are e-learning, information and learning technology (ILT), m-learning (mobile learning), blended learning, online learning and technology-enhanced learning. In some parts of the post-compulsory sector (e.g. further education colleges) the term ILT is often used but in others, e-learning or other expressions are employed. For the sake of simplicity I have chosen to use the term e-learning as a general one covering the others. The definitions of the different approaches are not always consistent and in some cases you might include aspects of several methods.

Example

Using an Internet-enabled mobile phone (iPhone) to participate in an online forum could be termed either m-learning since a mobile device is involved, online learning as online facilities are being used or blended learning if it was part of a face-to-face course.

Technology is continuously developing and its use in education and training is also growing rapidly. It is important to gain a sound foundation of skills and understanding that you can develop over your career in the same way that your teaching skills will be enhanced through experience and continuous professional development (CPD).

Benefits of e-learning

Many benefits of e-learning have been reported. Clarke (2008) emphasises that e-learning can allow learners considerable freedom to study, i.e. when, where and at their chosen pace. In addition he identifies the following benefits:

- Organising and storing your work
- Presenting your learning
- Analysing information
- Creating content

- Accessing information
- Capturing evidence of competency.

The Joint Information and Systems Committee (JISC) (2009a) provides a list of additional benefits that includes:

- Round-the-clock access to materials
- Different and more flexible ways of studying
- Working with others in dispersed locations
- Enhancing opportunities to reflect
- Quick feedback
- Improving active learning
- Enhancing learning communities.

The Learning Skills Improvement Service in their Policy Update 6 (2010) reported that one of the six key points that the Association of Learning Providing made to the Government Skills Minister in order to 'drive up quality whilst reducing unnecessary costs in FE' was 'the better use of e-learning and other 21st century IT solutions'.

Activity 1.2 Benefits of e-learning

Benefits are often very personal, so consider your own teaching and learning and decide which of the reported benefits are most appropriate to you. Also search the World Wide Web for other lists of benefits to ensure that you have considered all of them.

Trends in e-learning

In a dynamic and rapidly changing area such as technology, it is important to be aware of trends in e-learning and also what the research evidence is showing to be effective. The latter is vital since there are often pressures to adopt the latest product or approach. The key question is to ask yourself if it will enhance the learning experience. The British Education and Communication Technology Agency (Becta) has produced a variety of reports and articles on new emerging technologies that were previously available on their website at http://emergingtechnologies.becta.org.uk/. The Becta website closed on 31 January 2011 but its contents are available from the National Archives (http://nationalarchives.gov.uk/). In addition, Futurelab (http://www.futurelab.org.uk/) focuses on the innovative use of technology in education and has many developments underway to consider the possibilities that new developments will bring to learning. In higher education, the JISC supports many projects that investigate the possibilities of technology. Some of its projects are undertaken in further education colleges. JISC publications are available on its website at http://www.jisc.ac.uk/.

Activity 1.3 Trends in e-learning

Visit the Futurelab, Becta Emerging Technologies (now archived) and JISC websites and identify some trends in the use of technology in learning. In my case I identified:

1. 4G mobile phones
2. New interface technologies
3. Virtual reality
4. Transforming learning spaces
5. Repositories of digital content
6. Open access to learning materials.

Your own list will be different because the sites will have changed since I visited them.

Learning skills for e-learning

The impact of technology on society has been significant and continues to change the way people live. We have a generation of young people entering post-compulsory education who have grown up in a world in which information and communication technology (ICT) has been a normal part of their lives. They have attended schools in which technology has played a role in their learning and many young people see technology as a natural part of their lives using mobile phones, employing social networks and shopping online. This demonstrates a confidence in using technology that will obviously benefit them in e-learning. However, to benefit from e-learning requires not only technical skills but also learning skills. Clarke (2008) suggests that a successful e-learner is characterised by:

- Being a successful and confident independent learner especially in informal locations (e.g. home)
- Having a positive attitude to learning
- Being self-motivated
- Having good communication skills

- Being able to collaborate and co-operate with peers
- Being a competent user of technology.

Many e-learning approaches place an emphasis on learners working independently with the teacher's role being more of a facilitator or moderator than a presenter of information. It is therefore important that learning skills are well developed and can be combined with technical confidence to achieve the learners' objectives. It can be difficult to know which learners have the required combination to succeed in e-learning. Teachers should aim to develop their students' required learning skills.

Activity 1.4 Independent learner

A key role for teachers employing e-learning is to help learners to develop their learning skills. Consider your own context. How would you encourage the development of an independent learner? How could technology assist the process?

Digital literacy

Futurelab (2010) has published a handbook to help develop the skills required to fully participate in a digital society. The main target for the handbook is children, but the analysis of what is needed to become digitally literate applies to all ages and assisting learners to acquire the mix of skills and understanding is part of all learning programmes. The use of technology in learning is clearly a key aspect of developing digital literacy.

Futurelab (2010) has identified the following components that make up digital literacy:

- Functional skills (i.e. English, Mathematics and ICT skills and understanding)
- E-safety
- Effective communication
- Finding and selecting information
- Collaboration
- Cultural and social understanding
- Critical thinking and evaluation
- Creativity.

These areas are integrated across the different chapters.

Post-compulsory sector contexts

The post-compulsory or lifelong learning sector is complex, with many different groups of learners (e.g. offenders, young people and adult learners) studying for a wide range of programmes that include vocational qualifications, leisure and literacy. Courses can be either full- or part-time, with learning taking place in a variety of settings such as purpose-built colleges, community locations, workplaces and prisons. The availability and access to technology varies considerably across the sector. In a prison there are strict rules to limit access to certain types of technology based on security considerations while many colleges offer extensive access to technology but also restrict learners from participating in certain activities (e.g. social networks). The limitations are often based on ensuring the safety of learners. Teachers working in community locations will often only have access to whatever technology they can transport to the site, thus mobile and portable equipment is key.

How to use the book

The book has a range of activities covering all aspects of e-learning and you will gain the most from the book by undertaking as many as you can. Many relate directly to your own practice, such as suggesting that you ask your learners, as part of the induction process, to tell you about their technology experience, what technology they have access to and how they would like to use it within their studies. Some of the activities would be appropriate CPD actions to help develop your skills and understanding. In addition to the activities there are practical examples considering technology and its application, intended to demonstrate useful practice in e-learning. It is always important to reflect and review your use of e-learning so that your skills and understanding grow.

There are lists of resources and e-learning tools at the end of the book along with a glossary of terms.

Summary

The main points of this chapter are:

- This is a practical introduction to using technology in teaching and learning for experienced, newly qualified and student teachers.
- Staff in the post-compulsory sector are known by several different names but in order to simplify the language, the term teacher will be used throughout the book to cover names such as teacher, trainer and instructor.
- The contents of the book are related to the LLUK professional standards.

- There are many terms used to describe the application of technology in education and training. They include e-learning, ILT, m-learning, blended learning, online learning and technology-enhanced learning.

- E-learning can provide learners with the freedom to study when and where they choose and at their preferred pace.

- Technology is continuously developing so it is important to be aware of the trends to identify its potential to assist learning.

- A successful e-learner needs to have a range of skills, including acceptance of responsibility for their learning.

- To participate successfully in e-learning requires that learners are digitally literate.

- The post-compulsory sector is complex including many different types of learners, locations, technologies and contexts (e.g. adult learning, offenders, further education and work-based learning).

- The book includes activities, examples, lists of tools and resources. The more you employ these, the more you will gain.

2

Professional Values and Practice

Teaching standards (LLUK, 2007)

The standard statements AS1 to AS7 with the associated technology elements A1.1 to A7.1 Technology are covered in this chapter. These are not simply focused on the individual learner but include a community and even a global context. They consider the role that technology can play in increasing participation. Several of these aspects are also addressed in later chapters.

Introduction

E-learning is a dynamic and extensive subject covering various approaches such as:

- Face-to-face learning in the classroom
- Distance learning
- Learning on the move using mobile technology
- A combination of face-to-face learning, distance learning and learning on the move.

You need to consider what you are trying to achieve through the use of technology. Are you seeking to present content, engage learners, offer additional opportunities for communication or some other activity? Your objective will determine your choice of technology and approach. Simply deciding to employ technology because it is different will rarely be effective.

PRACTICAL EXAMPLE – ENGAGE LEARNERS

The electronic whiteboard provides various ways of improving the presentation of information in a classroom. However, it also has huge potential for engaging learners through asking small groups to use it to present the outcomes of a joint project, for discussion or for presenting some other group activity to the whole class.

Learners needs and background

Choosing which e-learning approach to employ also requires consideration of the learners' needs, background and familiarity with technology. It is important to consider the learners' own preferences in the use of technology, often called, in the singular, the learner's voice. The key questions are:

- What technology do they have access to?
- What technology are they motivated to use for learning?

Examples

1. Most people now have access to a mobile phone and text messaging is a communication method that almost everyone can employ. This allows you as the teacher, tutor or trainer to text your learners, sending messages of assessment reminders, changes in arrangements and updates to the course. The almost universal access to this technology gives you the assurance that your message will be received by the entire learning group.

2. The college or provider may offer learners an e-mail address but will they all use it? Many will prefer to use their own e-mail addresses and so may not read the college or provider's message. However, if the central e-mail source will re-direct mail to individual addresses then it is an effective way of communicating with learners with the additional advantages over text messages that messages can be longer and attachments can be included.

The JISC has supported a range of projects that consider the learner's voice and its importance in e-learning. These projects have shown that it is important to understand what learners' expectations of technology are, what technology they have access to and how they would want to use it. The JISC has produced a variety of guides, videos and other publications (JISC, 2009b).

Activity 2.1 Learner's voice

As part of the induction process to your course, ask the learners about their technology experience, what technology they have access to and how they would like to use it within their studies.

Teachers' e-learning experience

A second factor to be aware of, in addition to the learner's voice, is your own experience of e-learning. It is useful to have practical experience of online learning, developing an e-portfolio, writing a blog, e-mail discussion groups or one of the many other e-learning methods and approaches. This will allow you to put yourself in the place of the learners and know how they feel. It is important that you take advantage of any opportunities to participate as an e-learner.

Activity 2.2 E-learning experience

The Institute for Learning provides members with access to an online e-portfolio called Reflect. This enables you to experience developing a portfolio through selecting evidence of your CPD, receiving feedback on evidence from peers and teachers and then reflecting on the experiences and other associated activities. Take advantage of this opportunity to gain first-hand experience.

E-learning widening contexts (A2.1 Technology)

The creation of global education and training institutions is already underway, with many universities offering online courses for students living anywhere in the world. In addition, multinational companies are using online technologies to provide training and development opportunities without the need for international travel. As well as attracting learners from around the globe, these programmes also allow teachers to be based anywhere. This provides huge possibilities and challenges, such as working with multicultural groups that have different educational and training backgrounds. Technologies that are removing the barriers to global, community and personal engagement include:

- Social networking – sharing ideas
- Blogs – reflection
- Wikis – collaborative working
- Communication through chat, instant messaging, e-mail and discussion forums.

For the teacher, online methods require a change in approach from the role of a provider of knowledge to one of moderation and facilitation, although the former is still an important aspect.

Moderating and facilitating online programmes

Moderation can be considered in several ways, such as the simple maintenance of the discussion between students ensuring that it remains positive and constructive. This is a clear role but quite limited, and in some courses learners are asked to undertake it themselves. Teachers are more often needed to facilitate the discussion so that it probes the issues and achieves some depth. This is achieved through a variety of means, often similar to those employed in face-to-face discussion, such as asking a question to direct attention to a particular aspect that is being neglected. However, while a face-to-face activity is unlikely to last more than an hour or two, online discussions may continue for weeks. Due to the asynchronous nature of the medium, complex interaction patterns can develop (e.g. learners are free to comment on earlier messages and therefore return the discussion to an earlier issue). In addition, all participants have the freedom to contribute when it fits into their studies making it difficult to get the whole group participating at all times.

Salmons (2004) provides a model for moderation to help online groups develop a learning environment. Her model consists of five stages:

1. Access and motivation – moderation and facilitation encourages the learners to investigate the environment and introduce themselves.
2. Socialisation – moderation seeks to help the learning group to form.
3. Information exchange – learners are encouraged to share information and work together.
4. Knowledge construction – learners start to control their development of understanding and communication exchanges become deeper and more useful.
5. Development – individual learners and the group start to take responsibility for their development.

Activity 2.3 Moderation

Consider the Salmons five-stage model and identify what action you might take to successfully develop an effective online learning group with learners from many different communities.

Widening participation (A3.1 Technology)

Many learners encounter substantial barriers to their participation through disability or family responsibilities. Assistive and adaptive technologies can often significantly reduce barriers and enable students to learn when it most suits them. Many colleges and other education and training providers offer virtual learning environments (VLEs) through which learners can access learning materials and other resources at any time and from anywhere. This open access can be combined with technologies such as those that convert text to speech or speech to text, plus screen readers and voice recognition that allow disabled learners to participate.

Any technology that can be used by disabled learners to help them study can be considered as assistive and adaptive. The LExDis (Disabled Learners' Experiences of E-learning) project at Southampton University has created an online database of disabled learners' experiences (LExDis, 2010). The database is especially valuable in that it is disabled learners who are suggesting the approaches for other disabled learners.

Activity 2.4 LExDis database

Explore the LExDis database and website (http://www.lexdis.org/) for ideas that you could use in your own environment.

Activity 2.5 Experience

The world of a disabled student is substantially different and you will gain considerable insight into the issues encountered by these learners if you have experience of using assistive and adaptive technologies. Set yourself the challenge of:

1. Using voice recognition software to write a document
2. Accessing and navigating a website through a screen reader
3. Using alternative input devices
4. Employing any other technologies that your learners are using.

Supporting learners with technology

Technology can support learners' needs in a number of ways:

- Use Microsoft Windows accessibility options to:
    - Magnify the display
    - Change the size of text and icons
    - Convert the text displayed into speech (i.e. narrator)
    - Change the contrast
    - Display an onscreen keyboard
    - Convert the mouse for left-handed use.
- Deliver learning through an audio podcast rather than written handouts for visually impaired learners.
- Increase the character size on handouts for visually impaired learners.
- Adjust background colours and fonts to assist dyslexic learners.

■ Provide feedback on written work using the comments facility and track changes rather than handwritten notes, so that the learners can change character size or use a text to speech application to hear feedback.

Technology can often be used to support individual needs but used inappropriately it can become an obstacle. Staff need to be aware of the possibilities of technology and where to seek support to use it effectively. The Special Educational Needs and Disability Act 2001 (SENDA) (Office of Public Sector Information) has extended the Disability and Discrimination Act (DDA) into education. Providers must not act 'less favourably' towards disabled learners and must 'offer reasonable adjustments' which will ensure that disabled learners are not substantially disadvantaged in relation to those who are not disabled.

There are a variety of ways of using technology to assist learners. Techdis, an advisory service established to support learners in higher and further education, offers many publications, such as the Accessibility Essentials series, which help teachers' practice become more effective through technology. It frequently provides workshops and presentations at conferences and other events and offers an excellent website. Whilst they are a key resource, it is highly likely that your own college or provider will have specialist staff or services to help you as well.

Activity 2.6 Sources of support

This is a two-step activity:

1. Locate any support service within your college or provider and find out what help it can give you.
2. Visit the Techdis website at http://www.techdis.ac.uk/ and identify any publications or other information that would help you.

PRACTICAL EXAMPLE – IMPROVING PRESENTATIONS (TECHDIS, 2007)

You can often make your teaching and training more accessible by taking relatively straightforward steps such as in the examples below:

1. Use the notes field in Microsoft PowerPoint to explain any visual material included in your slides so that learners using screen readers can gain an understanding of what your are presenting.
2. Use hyperlinks to provide alternative slides so that learners can see the same content provided in a different way.

Accessibility Essentials 3 Creating Accessibility Presentations is available from Techdis and contains a wealth of practical suggestions.

Teachers roles in e-learning (A4.1 Technology)

Perhaps the first step in using technology to improve your ability to reflect on your experience and evaluate your own work is to understand how e-learning can support different aspects of teaching and training. This will provide a foundation on which you can compare your own use of technology.

E-learning is often linked to:

■ Active learning
■ Collaboration and co-operation
■ Reflection.

This requires an environment with opportunities to solve problems, to create materials, to work with others and for learners to be active. Your role is more likely to be a facilitator, moderator, mentor and coach than the traditional teacher who is imparting knowledge. However, part of your role will still be that of the traditional tutor explaining concepts, giving feedback and presenting information. Tait (n.d.) described in a case study the change in her teaching role using the term 'translator' in that she needed to help learners using ICT to research topics to understand what they had located.

The facilitator's role is focused on support and guidance (e.g. offering alternative approaches to learners) and providing a resource for the learners. The moderator's role is often linked to online forums or conferences. The moderator helps, encourages, supports and guides the learners' interaction. A mentor is usually an experienced person who can advise and discuss issues that concern the individual. Coaches aim to develop the individuals' performances by carefully reflecting with them on their efforts and offering guidance on specific aspects. Your own role may combine aspects from all these. In seeking to gain the benefits of e-learning you will need to develop your role as a facilitator, moderator, mentor or coach. Perhaps a useful first step is to consider whether you are combining a change of role from the traditional imparter of knowledge alongside your increasing use of technology. A common criticism is that the benefits of e-learning are not being achieved because the teachers are not changing their role to complement the technology.

Activity 2.7 Roles

Consider your approach to teaching or training and identify how far it could be described as:

■ Supportive
■ A guide
■ Being a resource
■ Encouraging

- Advisory
- Reflector.

There is no simple equation that tells you which aspects to emphasise. This will depend on your own context and objectives. However, if your role has not changed or is not changing alongside your use of technology perhaps you are not gaining all the benefits that e-learning can provide.

Direct delivery of information

E-learning can also assist with direct delivery through instruction or presentation of information. Hartley (1998) listed some principles for instruction based on cognitive psychology. Instruction should be:

- Well-organised
- Clearly structured
- Presented in a meaningful way, using appropriate language and context
- Able to relate new content to previous learning
- Taking into account the differences between individuals
- Structured to provide feedback to learners
- Focused on understanding.

Technology provides many aids to achieving these principles such as:

- Word processing of handouts and worksheets to provide high-quality structured materials
- Multimedia to improve meaningfulness and offer a clear context for content
- Capturing evidence (i.e. digital photographs showing practical skills) for enhancing feedback
- Providing content in alternative forms to offer learners more choice.

You need to consider if you are using technology to improve your instruction or simply replacing one approach with another. There is little difference between writing on a blackboard and using an electronic whiteboard if you are simply presenting text.

Activity 2.8 Instruction

Consider your approach to using technology to achieve Hartley's principles. What are the strengths and weaknesses of your methods?

Your teaching or training approach is governed by the learning objectives that you are aiming to achieve, the size of the group, the subject being taught and the available time. You need to consider these factors in deciding which are the most appropriate methods to employ.

Reflecting on your experiences

In teacher and tutor training, reflection has been identified as a professional practice that you should use both during initial training and also as part of continuous professional practice. It is important in determining which e-learning methods to select and how to use them, particularly in evaluating practice so that you can improve your approach. Figure 2.1 shows a model of how reflection can be facilitated by an e-portfolio. The Institute for Learning also provides all members with access to their Reflect e-portfolio thus offering a means of gathering evidence of professional development and reflection on your practice.

There are other ways that technology can be used to support reflection, including blogs and wikis. Blogs can be used to produce a reflective diary that can be shared with peers or even the whole world. Peers can add comments to blog entries so that a dialogue takes place. This can be a powerful means of considering approaches and personal development. Micro-blogging, based on technologies such as twitter, allows ideas, views and experiences to be shared with peers. This can take a variety of forms, such as a type of work shadowing.

Wikis provide the means to work collaboratively with other tutors and trainers to create a joint document, thus enabling members of a group to consider their use of technology. This could take a number of forms such as:

- Agreeing the strengths and weaknesses of different approaches
- Mapping the group's joint experience of e-learning
- Developing a strategic document.

PRACTICAL EXAMPLE – REFLECTION

Reflection is more than simply thinking about your experience. It requires a systematic approach and a degree of self-discipline. You might need to consider your positive and negative experience of e-learning, contemplate your feelings and question yourself. Reflection requires that you review, analyse and decide on improvements in the context in which you are working. Reflection requires practice and you will only improve your skills by undertaking it.

Professional development (A5.1 Technology)

Many professionals find that they learn most when working with or listening to the experiences of colleagues. Communication technologies now provide the means to collaborate with peers from both your own employer and the wider community. It is as easy to contribute to an international online forum as a local one. Probably the most employed method is the e-mail forum or conference in which if you send a message to a specific address, everyone who subscribes to the group receives it. There are many examples in the post-compulsory education sector of online forums being used to support the use of e-learning. The Regional Support Centres provide many local groups while Becta and the JISC offer national ones. Your own college or provider may well support in-house discussion groups.

These forums provide opportunities for you to share practice with peers and e-learning specialists. You can easily and effectively exchange materials and ideas and discuss new developments through conference groups. In addition to e-mail forums, technology offers other ways of assisting co-operation and collaboration such as:

- Google Docs – to enable a group of people to work on a shared document
- Twitter – to allow you to share and read about the experiences of other practitioners
- Blogs – to discuss and reflect on your experience
- Wikis – to collaborate on a common project.

There are lots of ways of working with your colleagues, either locally or at a distance. In fact, so many groups and possibilities exist that you will need to be selective about which ones are most appropriate for you.

PRACTICAL EXAMPLE – CONTRIBUTION

You will undoubtedly gain most from the groups to which you contribute most. This applies with face-to-face meetings and it is certainly true of online discussions and collaborations. Lurking or simply asking a few questions will not help you to develop as much as when actively contributing your own views and understanding.

Activity 2.9 Participation

Visit the Regional Support Centre, Becta or JISC and locate an e-mail forum or other collaborative groups. Join the group and participate as often as you can while maintaining a diary of your experiences to help you reflect on your approach to the group. What is the most effective way for you to participate?

Codes of practice and legal requirements governing the use of technology (A6.1 Technology)

The age of technology has brought with it the need for new laws to protect individuals from the associated risks. Your organisation will have developed codes of practice and policies to ensure that the legal requirements are fulfilled, that learners are protected and that facilities are not misused. You need to be aware of how these may impact on you and on your personal responsibilities to help maintain a safe learning environment. Some of the key areas are:

- Data protection
- Copyright and licensing
- Health and safety in relation to using technology
- Using technology appropriately
- Understanding the risks of viruses and malware
- Protecting learners.

Data Protection Act

The Data Protection Act provides the legal requirements for safeguarding personal information. You need to be aware of your role in ensuring learners' information such as marks, personal circumstances, disabilities and the many other details that a teacher and a learner may share are secure. Your organisation will probably have established procedures to safeguard information, such as regular changing of passwords, encrypting data and preventing personal information from being copied. Your responsibility is to follow the organisation's policies or to suggest improvements if you feel they are inadequate. There have been numerous examples of personal information being lost by staff not following their organisation's rules. It is unfortunately very easy to lose a memory stick and often too easy to copy sensitive information on to one.

Copyright

A huge advantage of the World Wide Web is access to the enormous quantity of information that it holds. While this is a major benefit to education and training, it also brings the risks of breaching copyright and plagiarism. Many people believe that material published on a website is free to use. In many cases this is true but only because the owner has chosen to allow you to use it. Most content is owned by someone who is able to decide on its use. You need to check the copyright conditions of the information. These are often displayed on the site. In some cases, copyright owners will allow materials to be used for educational purposes provided that no profit is made. In other cases, there is a licence given that may involve organisations and individuals paying a fee (e.g. e-journals). Learners who misuse copyrighted content are not only committing an illegal act but may also involve their organisation in the offence.

Plagiarism

Plagiarism is often a significant cause for concern when learners are using online sources. It is without doubt a major issue and plagiarism has quite probably increased with the use of web resources. However, plagiarism is now straightforward to control and check using online systems. The JISC supports the Plagiarism Advice Service (http://www.jiscpas.ac.uk/index.php) to assist teachers tackle the problem.

Activity 2.10 Plagiarism

Review the JISC activities and services to help combat plagiarism at http://www.jisc. ac.uk/whatwedo/services/academicintegrity.aspx and identify what help they can provide.

Health and safety

The use of technology has associated health and safety aspects such as:

- Repetitive strain injury
- Risk of tripping and falling
- Eye strain.

You have a duty of care to you learners to keep them safe. Your organisation will almost certainly have policies and codes of practice in relation to health and safety. There may also be specialist staff who can advise you.

PRACTICAL EXAMPLE – OUTREACH

There are occasions when you may be working in community-based locations as part of outreach programmes. It is important in these cases to undertake a risk assessment of the venue. You may have to use portable equipment that requires the use of extension cables or perhaps employ tables and chairs that are not intended to be used with computers. The degree of risk may well be higher in an outreach site than in a purpose-built facility. It is important to assess the situation and remove any hazards.

Acceptable use policy

With any equipment comes the associated problem of misuse. It is now common-place for education and training providers to have 'an acceptable use' policy. This will probably define the limits as to what the individual may employ the organisation's equipment to do. This can often cover a very wide range of activities from partici-pation in online groups (e.g. netiquette) to preventing the system being infected by virusses. There are many issues associated with acceptable use, including that of the learner's own equipment. Many people now have a range of portable ICT devices such as MP3 players, smartphones, netcomputers and digital cameras. In many ways, these could be effectively used to aid learning (e.g. listening to podcasts), but never-theless they also bring with them issues of acceptable use. Close, Hesse and De Cicco (2009) provide an example acceptable use policy for the National Institute for Adult Continuing Education (NIACE) Moodle VLE.

Activity 2.11 Own equipment

Consider the strengths and weaknesses of using the learners' own ICT technology. How would you ensure that its use is positive and that the learners do not misuse it?

Activity 2.12 Organisation policy and codes of practice

Find out what are your organisation's policies and codes of practice in relation to:

- Data protection
- Copyright and licensing
- Plagiarism
- Health and safety
- Acceptable use
- Virus and malware protection
- Safeguarding learning.

What are your responsibilities?

Safeguarding learners

Online methods that help tutors work together can also be employed to encourage learners to participate. However, you have a responsibility to safeguard your learners, and online group members are not always intent on helping other people but rather they prey on them. There are also legal aspects of accessing and downloading materials that might impact on your own organisation. *Safeguarding Learners in the Digital World* (Becta, 2009) provides an e-safety checklist for education and training providers of learners aged between 14 and 19 years old. It includes:

- Illegal downloading (e.g. copyright music)
- Plagiarism
- The implications of sharing private content on social networks
- Acceptable use of providers' facilities.

There are many risks for users of online technology. Your organisation is likely to have established policies to minimise the risks and you need to be aware of them. Ofcom (2009) have published 'Managing your Media' to help parents protect their children.

Teaching and learning approaches (A7.1 Technology)

E-learning provides a large set of tools to apply to your teaching. This can often overwhelm teachers in that they need to identify how best to use the various methods and approaches for their own teaching. Because each subject has its own unique needs and pedagogy, it can be a substantial challenge to decide what are the best approaches for you. Table 2.1 identifies some of the benefits of different tools. Chapters 3 and 4 develop this area.

TABLE 2.1 Practical benefits of e-learning

TEACHING AND LEARNING	E-LEARNING TOOLS	BENEFIT
Presentation of information	Electronic whiteboard	A focus for the learners that will hold their attention
	Video projector	Allows you to employ multimedia to enrich the presentation and motivate the learners
	Microsoft PowerPoint	Assists you by providing notes and handouts in addition to helping present information Slides are easy to revise and update
Handouts	Word processing	Straightforward way of producing a quality handout that is quick to amend and update Distribute handouts on college VLE or by e-mail
	Desktop publishing	Provides the means of producing a high-quality publication combining text and images Distribute publication on college VLE or by e-mail
	VLE	Provides access to course materials
	Image editors	Create an image to meet the precise needs of your learners Distribute images on college VLE or by e-mail

TABLE 2.1 (continued)

TEACHING AND LEARNING	E-LEARNING TOOLS	BENEFIT
Feedback	Camera	Offers the means to provide visual feedback (e.g. manual skills, dance and sports techniques)
	Annotation of electronic assignments	A means of providing specific feedback
	Quiz	Allows learners to self-assess
	Voting system	An interesting way of gaining insight into the views of a whole group
		Provides a catalyst for discussing a topic
Collaborative working	Wiki	Allows groups to work on a joint project asynchronously
	Google Docs	Provides the means for a dispersed group to work co-operatively
	Discussion forum	Allows a group to discuss issues and work together while separated in time and space
	Track changes in Microsoft Word	Offers a way of jointly writing and editing a report
Reflection	Blogs	Encourage learners to self-express and develop the skills to reflect on their experiences
Support and communication	E-mail	Allows learners and tutors to communicate outside of face-to-face sessions
		Discussion groups provide the means to share and debate ideas
	Text message	Short messages can be sent to keep learners informed of any administrative or other changes (e.g. reminders that an assignment is due)
	Twitter	Provides the means of shadowing individuals to gain an insight into their lives
	Instant messaging	Synchronous communication between individuals and small groups
	Skype	Synchronous means for individuals to communicate
Reinforcement	Interactive materials	Allows for individual practice to reinforce learning
Course materials	VLE	Provides:
		■ Easy distribution of learning materials ■ Access to course information ■ Access to library catalogues and online resources
Submission of assignments	E-mail attachment	Efficient and helpful to part-time and disabled students who do not need to travel to college to submit

The information in Table 2.1 shows that when applied to your subject and to learners, there are many benefits from different e-learning tools.

Activity 2.13 E-learning and your subject

Consider your own work and the range of approaches shown in Table 2.1. Select some methods that would be appropriate to your subject and reflect on the benefits that they may bring. You should also consider what you would need to do in order to achieve the desired outcome. For example:

- Using a digital camera to capture assessment evidence for a portfolio
- Employing a voting system to gain whole-class participation
- Annotating assignments using the word processing comments feature to provide formative feedback.

Technology also provides the means for you to assess your own efforts, enabling you to improve the quality of your teaching or training. The earlier sections have considered how technologies such as blogs and e-portfolios can help you reflect on your experiences. There are also approaches such as:

- Maintaining records of your work
- Analysing your learners' achievements to consider trends
- Comparing your experience with other colleagues.

Assessment (A1.1 Technology)

This section provides an introduction to assessment which is developed and extended in Chapter 6. There are several e-learning approaches that can help learners to assess and enhance their own progress. These include:

- E-portfolios
- Blogs
- Other forms of e-assessment.

E-portfolios

E-portfolios are electronic repositories of evidence of the learners' achievements. They can hold content in any format, including multimedia, and there is no limit to the quantity of material that a learner can store, nor for how long. Indeed, an e-portfolio can be used as a lifelong store of achievement. If this were the limit of the use of an e-portfolio, it would not be of great benefit. But this is just the beginning. Learners are able to use the collection purposefully and so aid their development by:

- Creating specific collections of evidence for particular purposes (e.g. to support a job application, for a course assessment or to produce a curriculum vitae (CV))
- Reflecting on the evidence so they can self-assess and review their own progress
- Sharing items with teachers and peers so they can provide feedback on their quality and value
- Producing learning plans based on analysis of the evidence
- Adding evidence from assessments.

Figure 2.1 illustrates a model of e-portfolio based learning (JISC, 2008) that is adapted from Kolb (1984). It shows that e-portfolios are not a passive approach to learning like filing evidence in a box but rather an active method that encourages learners to discuss, share, create, review, reflect and collaborate with others.

Learners can use their e-portfolios to review their progress and develop learning plans that will enable them to achieve their objectives. Several e-portfolio systems offer facilities for users to create individual learning plans, giving them a sense of ownership of their own learning. This is enhanced through the ability of the learners to reflect on their work and add these reflections to the evidence. Reflection as a means of achieving deep learning is seldom easy to achieve and requires practice and encouragement. Again, different systems provide reflective functions. Some offer a blog that can be used to produce a learning diary of experience or something similar. The blog can often be shared with peers or teachers so that reflections can be discussed and this will add value by providing feedback to the individual. The learner

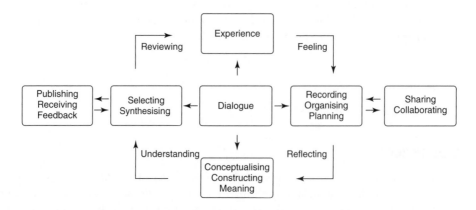

FIGURE 2.1 E-portfolio based learning model (JISC, 2008)

has control over who can access the blog so can choose to maintain a private diary or, alternatively, one that is widely available.

The simple existence of e-portfolio functions will not give learners the skills to utilise them effectively, so you will need to assist them to ensure they benefit from them. The e-portfolio needs to be integrated into the course of study so that the learners are motivated to use it. They must have as many opportunities as possible to develop the skills of selecting and classifying evidence, reflecting on their experiences, sharing material with peers and teachers and considering the feedback. A culture of collaboration is needed, ensuring that all members of the group will share content, reflect on feedback and support each other.

A range of e-portfolio products is available. Some are commercial systems while others are open source.

PRACTICAL EXAMPLE – E-PORTFOLIOS

It is important to emphasise the importance of selecting the most appropriate evidence and to encourage learners to classify each item so that they will be able to gather collections quickly to prove their competency, knowledge and skills in a specific context. Many e-portfolio systems provide the means to classify or tag items so that they can be grouped with similar items. The learners need to decide on their classification system or utilise one that relates to their occupation or another aspect of their lives. For example:

- Some key words or tags for an e-learning specialist are: online, blended, mobile, searching, moderate, wikis and blogs.
- These could form the classification of evidence to demonstrate e-learning skills and knowledge.

Reflection

An important learning skill is reflection. This is the ability to review systematically your experiences, comparing and contrasting them with other events and understanding. In this way, you can learn from your experience. It is a skill that is widely required in many professions. Reflection is a critical learning skill as it is a means of ensuring that deep learning takes place. It involves relating new facts to existing knowledge, questioning it, structuring knowledge and identifying its key points. It is about actively considering how new knowledge or experience relates and changes with context.

Several e-learning approaches can assist learners to reflect on their experiences:

- Using blogs to develop a form of online learning diary in which peers and tutors can send comments is often an effective way of encouraging reflection.
- Reflecting on learning activities, experience and evidence in e-portfolios can encourage reflection.
- Reflections can form part of e-mail discussion forums.

- Collaborative activities (e.g. developing a joint document using a wiki) can serve to encourage reflection.

Reflection is more than a simple description of an activity. It requires that learners analyse in relation to their previous experience. They will need help and support to develop their skills of reflecting, and the feedback of teachers and peers is often very useful. Some ways of helping learners to develop their skills are:

- Provide examples of reflection
- Offer advice and guidance on how to reflect
- Provide opportunities to reflect
- Give feedback on learners' reflections
- Integrate reflective activities into course activities.

Summary

The main points of this chapter are:

- E-learning is a dynamic and extensive subject covering many different approaches.
- Learners' own preferences, experiences and ownership of technology are critical to their effective use for learning.
- E-portfolios are electronic repositories of evidence that can serve a range of purposes (e.g. a lifelong store of achievement, a review of individual progress and assisting learners to reflect on their experiences).
- Reflection is a critical learning skill because it is a means of ensuring that deep learning takes place.
- Any technology that can be used by disabled learners to help them to study can be considered as assistive and adaptive.
- The use of technology in global education and training institutions is already underway with many universities offering online courses for students living anywhere in the world.
- The role of the tutor is changing from being a provider of knowledge to one of moderation and facilitation.
- Assistive and adaptive technologies can often significantly reduce barriers and enable students to learn when it most suits them.
- E-learning requires an environment of active learning, collaboration and co-operation and reflection.
- E-learning can also assist with direct delivery through instruction or presentation of information (e.g. word processing handouts and worksheets to provide high-quality structured materials).

- Communication technologies now provide the means to collaborate with peers from both your own employer and the wider community.

- Organisations have developed codes of practice and policies to ensure that the legal requirements associated with the use of technology are fulfilled, learners are protected and that facilities are not misused.

- E-learning provides a large set of tools to aid learning; the most appropriate for each subject and activity need to be selected.

Learning and Teaching

Teaching standards (LLUK, 2007)

The standard statements BS1 to BS5 with the associated technology elements B1.1 to B5.2 Technology are covered in this chapter. The focus is on using technology to enhance learning by improving communication, collaboration, motivation and learning skills. There are also relationships with the technology elements in Chapter 2 (i.e. A1.1 to A7.1).

Introduction

Technology can help you in a wide range of ways. It can assist you with learning and teaching by:

- Researching your subject
- Locating e-learning and other resources to integrate into your sessions
- Creating learning materials from the straightforward handout summarising the key points to producing interactive multimedia resources
- Extending your face-to-face sessions through communication technologies (e.g. e-mail discussion forums)
- Adding interest and flexibility through technology (e.g. electronic whiteboards)
- Improving formative and summative assessment (e.g. annotating assignment with feedback)
- Improving reflective skills (e.g. blogs)
- Assisting peer support (e.g. wikis).

There are probably many other applications of technology to learning and teaching and they are growing with each new technological development. It can be quite daunting to consider all the technological possibilities available to you. There are probably many more possibilities than you have the time or resources to pursue. You need to identify and concentrate on what your learning and teaching objectives are and which e-learning methods would be the most appropriate to employ to achieve your goals.

New technological and e-learning approaches are continuously being developed. You do not have to jump on every bandwagon but it is important to include technology in your CPD activities so that you are aware of the possibilities and are able to judge if a new development would be appropriate.

Activity 3.1 Improve

Consider your own teaching and list the main issues you would like to improve. For example:

1. Improve motivation and interest of learners in the subject
2. Encourage more peer support outside of the classroom
3. Improve personal presentation methods
4. Achieve better outcomes.

At the end of the chapter we will return to this activity and attempt to identify e-learning approaches that would help you address the issues.

Learning environments (B1.1 Technology, B2.3 Technology and B3.1 Technology)

Technology can help create both a learning environment that motivates and supports learners and one that is not limited to a physical classroom or the times of face-to-face sessions. It enables individuals to participate at the time, place and pace that they prefer. Technology can replace the classroom when used as a distance learning approach or extend the face-to-face sessions as part of a blended learning approach. However, e-learning is not a magic wand and its use needs to be carefully thought through. It requires skills and understanding to employ it effectively.

One of the most straightforward actions to extend the classroom learning environment is to get everyone to agree to share e-mail and mobile phone numbers. This allows the group to communicate between sessions. Nevertheless, this does not guarantee success since the learners will need a reason to communicate. Some ways of encouraging communication are:

- Encourage group work so that individuals can share ideas between face-to-face meetings.

- Use texts to keep the group up to date with course changes, deadlines and administration.

- Send handouts as e-mail attachments.

- Get responses from learners using Wallwisher (http://www.wallwisher.com) or a similar system that lets them post their views on an online notice board as part of an activity. The outcomes could serve as interesting content for classroom activity/discussion.

- Use Polleverywhere (http://www.polleverywhere.com/) or a similar system to obtain feedback from the learners about an issue. Polleverywhere allows them to send responses as text messages. The outcomes of the poll could be reviewed in class as a stimulus for discussion as well as encouraging communication.

The key is to integrate the approach into the course so that learners can easily see the relevance and benefits of participation.

Activity 3.2 Wallwisher (http://www.wallwisher.com)

Wallwisher is an online notice board where members of a group can post their views on an issue while being able to read the other comments. Visit the site and consider the demo wall. Consider how you might use Wallwisher to encourage a discussion about an issue linked to the course you are teaching.

Activity 3.3 Polleverywhere (http://www.polleverywhere.com/)

Polleverywhere is a system that allows learners to send their views on a subject by text message and to view the results in their browser or Microsoft PowerPoint. Visit the site and consider the examples. Consider how you might use Polleverywhere to encourage a discussion about an issue linked to the course you are teaching. One way would be to ask learners to respond in a face-to-face session to ensure immediate participation and then ask them to send further responses after the classroom discussion.

VLEs

Many education providers in the post-compulsory sector have implemented VLEs, sometimes also called learning management systems (LMSs). In colleges they are almost universally available although this is not true in other parts of the sector. Becta's 'Harnessing Technology Review 2009', published in 2010, reported that 92 per cent of further education colleges had a VLE in 2009 while only 32 per cent of work-based learning providers had access to one. In adult and community learning

VLEs were being implemented but the sector is just beginning to make effective use of the technology. VLEs vary in the facilities they offer but in many cases they provide facilities such as:

- Downloadable resources – handouts, course materials and other materials can be accessed by learners
- Course information – details about the course content, assessment and other administrative matters are available
- Discussion forums for each course – these allow learners to discuss issues between face-to-face sessions
- Access to library catalogues and online publications
- Links to blogs or wikis.

PRACTICAL EXAMPLE – MOODLE (HTTP://MOODLE.ORG/)

Moodle is an open source VLE. It can be freely downloaded from the Moodle Community website (http://moodle.org/). Its use has grown rapidly and it is widely employed in Great Britain across all educational sectors.

VLEs are potentially a powerful set of learning tools, but it does require effort to realise their possibilities. Simply providing a discussion group for your learners is unlikely to have a big effect. Learners will often ignore them unless they have reasons to use them. You need to decide what is their role in your teaching. For example, they are often effective in encouraging and achieving an increase in mutual peer support. Once you have decided what role you want the discussion group to serve, you need to integrate it into your course. Learners may have to be encouraged to use it. Some keys issues to achieve a successful group are:

1. Developing a supportive community – this can take time, several weeks or longer depending on the group and how integrated into the course is the discussion forum:

    a. It needs to be a warm, welcoming and positive place.

    b. Messages need to be responded to quickly and it is often useful to widen the topic by explaining related issues (in a sense you are adding value).

    c. Netiquette is critical, in that everyone needs to feel free to contribute without aggression.

2. Reasons for participation:

    a. Learners need a reason to participate – what is the benefit to them (e.g. to develop the skills of collaborating within a team)?

    b. Encourage message posting by making strong and useful links to the course (e.g. embed activities that require learners to work together).

    c. Group activities are often an effective way of developing communication.

In higher education, participation in the course discussion group is often assessed in order to make clear to learners that its use is important. That said, the key issue is to determine its role and give learners a powerful reason to be involved before you add assessment. If the only reason for taking part is the assessment then learners will often simply do just enough to satisfy the assessment and fail to gain the wider benefits.

Learners who read discussion group postings but who rarely add their own comments are called lurkers. While this is often seen as a negative type of behaviour, it does resemble that of quiet learners in a face-to-face class who can listen to answers to questions posed by their peers and therefore gain understanding. Lurking is therefore not necessarily poor practice for the individual learner, but if everyone lurked then no one would benefit.

Activity 3.4 Benefits

Consider your own teaching and what role a discussion forum could play. Identify the benefits to the learners of integrating one into the course.

The single most common use of a VLE is probably that of allowing learners to access course materials such as handouts, study guides and assignments. This may seem a minor use but it is useful to learners in that it adds more flexibility to the course. This is very important to the learner who has family commitments, so that if they miss face-to-face sessions they have the opportunity to access the notes and other materials from the VLE. Learners who speak English as a second language or learners with hearing impairments can often benefit from reading material in advance to prepare or after the session to review the content.

Supporting reflection

In post-compulsory education reflection is encouraged in many ways, including asking learners to keep a diary of their learning. Blogs provide a technological way of supporting reflection and learning diaries.

A blog is a website in which entries are presented in date order so that they form a type of diary. A blog can be a closed environment to which only the individual has access. However, this is likely to have limited benefits. A blog that is also open to the learner's peers, allowing them to add comments to the learner's entries, will extend its value considerably. It offers peer support and widens the scope of the reflections. Teachers can also add comments and again this adds value to the process.

Figure 3.1 shows a simple blog created with Blogger, a free tool provided by Google.

Blogs are not only limited to learning diaries but can also be used for any group interaction you require. They are simply a way of posting comments in date order from an individual or group so that they can support each other while exploring top-

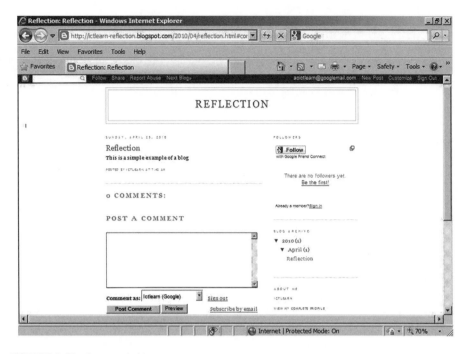

FIGURE 3.1 Simple example blog

ics and issues that are relevant to them. A tutor-controlled blog might take the form of your posting issues and asking your learners to comment on them in the same way that you might discuss them in a classroom. The advantage here is that the discussion can continue between face-to-face sessions and everyone is free to post. The discussion will not be dominated by the more extrovert members of the group.

While blog sites allow individuals to post substantial messages, twitter has been used as part of microblogging, which is sending short comments to a group of people who can respond in a similar way. This has been used to create learning networks with a group of learners studying the same subject and providing each other with support and assistance.

Activity 3.5 Blogs

Consider how a blog would contribute to your teaching (e.g. individual learning diaries to improve reflection skills, a mutual support environment or a discussion group). You might wish to consult your learners because they will only use it if they can understand its purpose and recognise its benefits to them.

Activity 3.6 Create a blog (https://www.blogger.com/)

Based on your analysis of needs from Activity 3.5 create a blog using Blogger or another system (i.e. your institution may provide blogs for learners' use).

Virtual classrooms

There are now several products that provide what is essentially a virtual classroom. They offer a variety of features such as:

- Presenting information through a shared whiteboard
- Video and audio conferencing
- A text channel so that learners can send texts to you and each other
- Sharing a computer desktop
- Quizzes and tests.

Figure 3.2 illustrates Elluminate, which is widely used in education for many different purposes including:

- Online conferences
- Individual and small group tutorials
- Seminars
- Staff training sessions
- Presentations.

Elluminate and other virtual classroom systems are synchronous technologies. This means that all participants are taking part at the same time. In order to use a virtual classroom you need to understand and be competent in using their functions and features. This requires moderating and facilitating a group by controlling who can participate through observation of the messages from learners (e.g. participants can signal that they want to contribute by using devices such as an electronic hand raise or sending a text message). This requires concentration and can be quite tiring over a long session. In my personal experience the most effective sessions are those that are highly participative and I have used the quiz features to encourage controlled participation successfully. In comparison, the virtual classroom does allow for presentations to large groups although it is often useful to have a team approach with one person concentrating on moderating the event while the other presents.

FIGURE 3.2 Virtual classroom system Elluminate (screen shot provided by the company)

Social networks

The initial use of personal computers (e.g. BBC B Microcomputer) was often based around the use of social groups. Small groups worked together on computer-based activities that centred around the computer itself. This encouraged them to improve their communication skills and learn to work in a team. The computer provided a focus for the group work. This is still true today with social networking encouraging communication and group working although now more often in a virtual space rather than face-to-face.

For a large proportion of the population social networks such as Facebook are a normal part of their lives. They allow users to maintain relationships with a wide range of friends and acquaintances. However, although many people are using social networks in their personal worlds it does not mean that they have experienced using them as part of their education. There are also safety issues involved in using social networks with the result that many institutions have barred access to them in order to safeguard their learners. However, an alternative to a bar is to create a closed social network for learners enrolled with the institution. There is a variety of tools available to create your own network such Ning (http://www.ning.com/), Elgg (http://elgg.org/) or SocialGo (http://www.socialgo.com/). These tools allow you to create a network that is specifically tailored to your needs and since you own the network, it is a safe environment for your learners. Alternatively, you can add a social dimension to your VLE by providing some discussion forums in which learners can socialise. Sometimes called a cafe or something similar, they often serve as a means for learners studying a range of courses to meet and talk.

Collaboration

A wiki is an application that allows a group to create an agreed document. Wikis are relatively simple to use and since all participants are free to edit the document and add new information, the group must come to an agreement. They maintain a record of changes so that all learners can identify who made each change. The approach encourages group collaboration and co-operation and so helps develop the required skills and attitudes. Wikis can be used for a wide range of purposes such as:

- Agreeing a project report
- Drawing up a project plan
- Identifying all the steps needed in a process.

The main limit is that wikis require a systematic approach to achieve a successful outcome so the group must agree to work together. Editing the information provided by another member of the group does require confidence and so wikis can become merely a list of inputs with little editing to bring them together if no one has the necessary confidence.

PRACTICAL EXAMPLE – GOOGLE DOCS SHARING

Google Docs provides a function to share content with other defined users, making it possible to create a group discussion forum that works both as a synchronous and asynchronous communication area. By opening the Google word processing application, the group can send messages and undertake the creation of a joint document. All the applications can be used in this way so it is potentially a powerful collaborative tool.

Discussion forums

A discussion forum is an asynchronous communication environment in which learners can send messages that other members of their group can read and respond to. They are widely used but it is often a challenge to create an effective community of learners. This is due to many factors such as:

- Asynchronous communication is very flexible and convenient but does require users to be self-disciplined in checking for new messages.
- Groups who meet each other regularly or have other means of communicating may prefer these methods to the forum. Learners need to see a benefit of using the forum.

Forums offer many advantages in that everyone is free to contribute to the discussions without the blocks that occur in face-to-face groups where some learners are reluctant to present their views. However, the communication method can result in misunderstanding since you cannot see the sender's body language. Netiquette needs to be carefully followed to avoid arguments. Asynchronous communication allows learners time to consider their answers which should help a more in-depth discussion take place. However, it can still be difficult to get everyone to participate. The moderator's role is to encourage learners to take part. Often a direct e-mail to learners, persuading them to join in, will be sufficient.

The forum provides a permanent record of the contributions enabling learners to review the whole exchange and this allows them to catch up if they have fallen behind. You can provide answers to queries that everyone can benefit from.

Forums have been extensively employed in education and training. While they offer many benefits, like most methods they are not perfect and do have disadvantages such as:

- Records of communication can make learners reluctant to send messages.
- Text-only communication can lead to misunderstandings.
- Group activities can lead to resentment if some learners have not contributed.

Activity 3.7 Forums

The teacher's role in a forum is to moderate and facilitate its operation. As the moderator you will often be able to carry out a range of activities to help the group work together. These include:

1. Deleting messages
2. Moving messages to new threads
3. Starting new discussion threads
4. Access to management statistics showing the use of the forum (i.e. you can see who has visited but not posted a message).

It is important to be aware of the functions and be able to use them. Visit your institution's forums and explore the options available to you.

Conferencing

Video discussion

By using a webcam or more complex equipment, it is possible to link two or more personal computers so that you can communicate with each other through vision and speech. This offers a powerful system for one-to-one tutorial support or with a larger group. It is effective if you have prepared for the session and manage the process. With a group of people it is important to agree an approach that allows each person to speak, otherwise the danger is that everyone tries to speak at the same time or learners get frustrated by being unable to contribute. You need to have prepared for the session and to chair it systematically.

Voice over Internet Protocol (VoIP) (e.g. Skype)

Telephone learning support has a long history of success in organisations such as the Open University. VoIP provides the means of conversing with people around the world at low cost. You can hold telephone conferences with several people but as with video conferencing, you need to prepare and manage the process in a systematically agreed way.

Voice recording

Digital sound recorders are now widely available making it possible to record conferences, lectures, interviews, group activities and other meetings. This is a means of creating a complete record of an event for a project or to assist disabled students. However, although recording does provide a comprehensive record, it does have an impact on the individual or group being recorded. People will often be less open and more careful in their responses. You must always seek their permission to record them. In addition, listening to a recording to identify the key issues can often take a long time compared to using handwritten notes.

Microblogging (e.g. twitter)

Blogging is often a person's reflections, views and ideas on a particular topic, published in date order. It is valuable in learning since it encourages the development of reflective skills and can allow peers and teachers to provide feedback. Microblogging aims to achieve similar goals but it involves the use of only short text messages. The limited nature of the messages may help the participation of learners who are discouraged by the longer communications in a blog. Microblogging can work well as a flow of experience with the learners providing a type of commentary on what they are doing (e.g. field trip and project activities). It thus encourages precise communication, reactions to new experiences and dialogue. Twitter is probably the most obvious way of undertaking microblogging with peers acting as followers. It is an immediate communication and can be undertaken while on the move or stationary.

Online learning environment support

The key to employing all online learning environments is adequate and appropriate support. This is often called moderation or facilitation but it is essentially a mixture of different actions such as:

- Balancing the need to encourage discussion without exerting too much control; the discussion group need to feel that they own the debate
- Appointing learners to act as moderators can signal that the group are in control and own the discussion

- Encouraging a deep discussion since online discussions will often remain relatively superficial without some assistance such as probing questions and suggesting issues to explore

- Encouraging participation (e.g. the direct e-mail to a learner who has not taken part can often identify problems that are stopping participation)

- Responding to questions quickly (e.g. learners often get frustrated if their requests are not answered almost immediately)

- Providing motivation (e.g. learners need a reason to join in)

- Ensuring netiquette is being followed by the whole group (e.g. everyone should have an equal opportunity to give their views without fear of being attacked by others)

- Regular attendance to check what is going on (e.g. reading the messages is often one of the most useful contributions since it will enable you to identify who is not participating and diagnose if you need to inject any stimulus)

- Creating activities to engage your learners (e.g. simply telling a group to discuss the course topics in a general way is unlikely to encourage involvement; you will need to create a distinct focus with outcomes that the learners can identify with and benefit from)

- Summarising discussions can often be very helpful especially when scores or hundreds of messages have been sent. It is often an opportunity to ask one of the group to be the summariser, again showing that it is their debate.

Activity 3.8 Participation

In online learning environments, there is little substitute for the practical experience of participating. It provides you with the opportunity to understand how a learner perceives the setting, a chance to observe moderators' and facilitators' methods and to communicate with peers. There are many ways of obtaining experience such as:

1. Enrolling in an online course (e.g. Open University)
2. Participating in online forums offered by the regional support centres (e.g. RSC West Midlands offers a wiki, RSC Yorks and Humberside provides access to a learning platform and RSC Wales offers a blog)
3. Taking part in an online conference
4. Many face-to-face events offer access from a distance by using webcams.

Try to gain some experience and reflect on the advantages and disadvantages of the different approaches.

Learners' motivation

Motivation of the learners is a key factor in all forms of education and training. Learners must be able to recognise the benefits of taking part in order to be motivated. E-learning provides a range of motivational benefits including:

- Flexibility – learners have more freedom to access learning at the time and place they prefer (e.g. VLEs, discussion forums, mobile learning and blogs)
- Communication – more opportunities for learners to exchange information and support each other through communication technology
- Independent learning – learners have more choice and responsibility
- Improved access for disabled learners
- A richer range of learning experiences to meet different learning preferences
- Encouragement to create and publish resources
- Assessment – it can be provided when learners want to undertake it
- Developing advanced skills such as self-reflection
- Teachers and managers have better access to learners' performance information.

Several reports and studies have indicated that learners with literacy and numeracy difficulties are often motivated to improve their skills and knowledge through the use of technology. As early as 2001, the Department for Education and Skills' national strategy *Skills for Life* stated that many adults with poor basic skills would be motivated through the use of computers. Clarke (2003) reported that the reading, writing and mathematics skills of learners had been improved through the use of technology.

It is also important to realise that for many young people who employ technology as a seamless part of their lives there is an expectation that technology will play a similar role in their education and training. If absent, it is likely to have a negative influence on their motivation. Technology is not a panacea, however. It needs to be used appropriately to achieve the best results and inappropriate use can actually de-motivate learners.

Finally, it is important to realise that not everyone will want to use all forms of e-learning equally. Some learners will prefer traditional methods (e.g. listening to a face-to-face presentation rather than watching a video of the session and reading a book in preference to searching the World Wide Web). It is therefore useful to offer learners as much choice as possible.

Learning environment approaches

The range of approaches that can form whole or part of a learning environment can seem bewildering. In normal circumstances you are unlikely to want to start using all of them at once. You need to select those that are most likely to meet the learners' needs and your objectives. It requires experience in many cases to obtain the benefits from any method. Table 3.1 provides a brief summary of a range of approaches.

TABLE 3.1 Benefits and limitations of learning environment approaches

APPROACH	POTENTIAL BENEFITS	LIMITATIONS	COMMENTS
VLE	VLEs allow a wide range of resources to be made accessible to the learners.	Learners need to be confident users in that they need to explore the environment to employ it effectively.	It is important to make learners aware of the possibilities and encourage their participation.
Discussion forum	Forums are flexible and convenient. Permanent record of the discussion is created. Asynchronous communication gives learners time to reflect before replying, so more in-depth discussion can take place.	Forums require users to be self-disciplined in checking for new messages. Recording of communication can make learners reluctant to send messages. Lack of participation by some learners can be resented by others.	Moderation is vital for success. They need to be confident users of the system and proactively encouraging participation. Netiquette needs to be agreed and followed. Activities need to be clearly defined and designed.
Virtual classroom	The virtual classroom offers a communication channel that is suitable for one-to-one, small and large group events. It is immediate in being synchronous communication and overcomes the barrier of a geographically distributed group. A very flexible resource that can meet a wide variety of needs. There are many functions (e.g. text chat, sharing presentations, video and audio communications).	Its obvious limit is that it is synchronous, so widely dispersed students in different time zones may find it difficult to participate.	Virtual classrooms provide a powerful learning tool. However, you will to need to invest time in learning how to use the rich range of functions and how to exploit them most effectively. With a large group it is sometimes effective to work with a partner so that one person can focus on presentation while the other maintains the communication channels.
Blog	Blogs offer the means to reflect on	Blogs require a well-motivated learner to	Learners may need help and support to

TABLE 3.1 (continued)

APPROACH	POTENTIAL BENEFITS	LIMITATIONS	COMMENTS
	experiences through critical and analytical writing.	maintain the regular inputs needed to gain their benefits.	develop a reflective writing style.
	Peer review and support can be provided through comments.	Blogs open to others may discourage less confident learners.	It is useful to provide guidance and include activities to develop necessary skills.
Social network	Social networks encourage participation; help develop communication skills and group working. They should therefore be a key tool for learning.	Individuals may see their involvement in social networks as part of their private lives and not wish to use them for education purposes. The limitation can be overcome by establishing separate social networks.	As with many tools learners need tasks and activities to exploit the potential of the social network.
Wiki	Wikis offer a way of encouraging collaboration and co-operation between learners. The wiki process helps learners to develop group working skills. The group can create joint outcomes. Wikis are flexible and can be used for a wide range of tasks.	To use a wiki successfully requires a systematic approach. Editing information requires confident learners.	Learners will often need a clear, well-designed task to employ the wiki effectively. You will need to allow learners time to become familiar with the application which, although straightforward, may be new to them. Learners need to be focused and organised users of the wiki.

Learners' safety (B1.1 Technology)

There is a clear responsibility on education and training providers to ensure the online safety of their learners. This can be done in many ways including merely excluding access to the wider Internet and social network sites from the institutions. Many colleges and other providers have barred access to some online resources in order to ensure the safety of their learners. However, this does not safeguard the learners' safety if they are working from home nor does it help them develop the skills and understanding to use facilities safely. It also removes the benefits that many online sites, resources and experiences can offer learners. Sharples et al. (2008) in a report for Becta stated that 'Safe Internet use requires balancing perceived benefits against acceptable risks.' The report's focus was on children at Key Stages 3 and 4. Learners in post-compulsory education come from a very wide range of ages and backgrounds but they do include people who are young and inexperienced, are vulnerable or are simply new to online technologies. These learners need to be safe and assisted to develop the skills and understanding to keep themselves secure.

Some key factors to keep yourself and learners safe online are:

1. Don't reveal personal data about yourself or other people to anyone you do not know (e.g. don't share personal information on a blog).

2. Don't post pictures that you would not like family or employers to see – many employers now search the Internet for details about applicants.

3. Keep passwords secure; do not reveal them to anyone.

4. Use the safety features available in many social networks to control access to your information.

5. Don't allow people to be listed as your friends on social networks when you don't know them.

6. Don't reply to any e-mails from people or organisations you don't know.

7. Don't write messages in any media (e.g. blogs, discussion forums and wikis) that are offensive in anyway. It is very poor practice; is also likely to be in breach of the conditions of use of the service and possibly illegal (i.e. defamation).

8. Don't download any material unless it is from an individual or site you know. You risk infecting your system with viruses, spyware and other unpleasant effects.

9. Keep your viruses and spyware applications up to date and use them to check all incoming messages.

Activity 3.9 E-safety resources

There are a number of resources available for teachers about e-safety, including materials to help you teach aspects of the subject. Carry out an Internet search to locate resources. You may find it useful to search the Excellence Gateway, Techdis, Webwise, Becta, JISC and the Regional Support Centres websites. Many are aimed at children but these can be adapted for older learners, and some cases materials are aimed at the post-compulsory sector.

As a teacher you may well use social networking sites and communication networks such as twitter in your private life. However, remember that anything you post online may be accessed by your learners, colleagues and employers.

Netiquette

Netiquette is a set of rules that govern individual behaviour in online environments. These rules are very important in providing a framework within which learners can participate without anxiety. Educational institutions will often provide a set of rules but it can be effective to ask groups to define their own. They are often more motivated to obey their own rules than those set by an institution.

Activity 3.10 Netiquette

Ask a group of learners to consider what rules should govern their collaboration and co-operation while undertaking online activities. Compare their conclusions with your own netiquette conditions. Learners will frequently set more stringent rules than an educational provider.

Independent learning (B2.2 Technology)

Society has already evolved into one that places communication and information technologies at its centre. The majority of people are using the Internet as their main source of information encouraged by business, government, community and education, which are all employing technology as their main windows to the world. Tait (n.d.), in a comparison of two groups of hairdressing learners, one using ICT to complete assignments and the other paper, concluded that the ICT learners achieved better results and that this was in part due to their improved learning-to-learn skills. The potential for learners to become more independent is clearly apparent through technological developments such as:

- Using the Internet to research subjects
- Listening to podcasts from experts on the move with MP3/MP4 players
- Capturing sound and video with hand-held cameras or mobile phones
- Accessing websites from anywhere with personal digital assistants (PDAs) and smart phones
- Creating learning journals to reflect on experience
- Recording notes electronically
- Submitting and presenting high-quality assignments.

There are many more examples that illustrate the potential for individuals to become independent learners. However, the existence of the technology means that to achieve independence is not on its own sufficient. Individuals require both the technical skills and also the associated learning skills to gain the benefits. Some of the learning skills required for independent learning were shown in Chapter 1.

Independence means that learners have the freedom to choose when and where they learn. This means they must be skilled in taking responsibility for their studies and managing their time. Technology applications can help them create study plans by using Microsoft Outlook or Google Calendars. The teacher can assist by offering feedback and support in producing plans.

Independence means being able to undertake research. This means not merely having search skills but, more importantly, being able to judge the quality of sources and information they hold. The teacher can assist by helping to develop these skills, which are sometimes called information literacy.

Communication skills are key to gaining independence. Can you write clear and succinct messages using no more than the 140 characters that twitter provides? Even e-mail places an emphasis on short, focused statements. Asynchronous communication technology can easily result in having to manage many messages every day. It is not easy and if, in addition, you are using synchronous communications then the complexity and pressure will increase. How can a teacher assist learners to develop the right skill sets in an environment where they may be balancing several e-mail accounts, instant messaging, texting, participation in online discussion forums and maintaining a blog? One way to minimise this complexity is by considering your own course design so as to reduce learners' stress and to concentrate on the most important approaches in your context.

Many employers place considerable value on employees who can work in a team, collaborating and co-operating with the other members. In learning, collaboration and co-operation are equally important aspects. To develop these skills requires practice. You can contribute to their development by designing your courses to provide suitable opportunities for the learners.

Activity 3.11 Communication technology

Consider what your course requires from your learners as well as the systems and technology they are already employing in their private lives. Decide which are the most important to successful study in your context and focus the design of the course around them.

Feedback

Probably the most effective way a teacher can assist the development of independence is through feedback. Technology provides a range of ways of offering learners feedback, such as using the comment and track changes features available in Microsoft Word. You can add your views and relate them directly to the learners' efforts. Figure 3.3 illustrates the use of the comment function.

The annotated digital document can be returned quickly to the individual. Blogs provide the opportunity to offer comments on the individual's reflections. Feedback is recorded so that learners can review it several times (e.g. during revision for assessment).

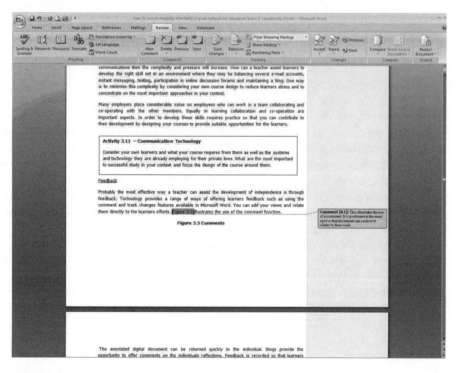

FIGURE 3.3 Microsoft Word's comments feature

There are many good sources of advice on the most effective ways of giving feedback. Some suggestions are:

- Balance your comments between the strengths and weaknesses of the work. Positive comments will encourage learners while negative can be destructive.

- Constructive feedback that helps the learners understand what they must do to improve is vital.

Informal learning

The Oxford Internet Survey (Dutton, Helsper and Gerber, 2009) reported that in 2009, the use of the Internet for informal learning had grown to 91 per cent of users who had checked a fact online, 90 per cent who investigated something of personal interest and 71 per cent who had sought the definition of a word. The World Wide Web is the now the information source of choice for most people and it therefore has enormous potential for personal education. However, it is difficult to link informal to formal learning (Schuller and Watson, 2009). One way is to realise that learners may well have developed useful informal learning skills that we should encourage in formal settings. It is easy to dismiss informal learning as not having anything to contribute to formal, qualifications-linked learning. This would be a mistake. Employers are seeking staff who can innovate, be self-starters and are independent learners. You should encourage learners to take responsibility for their own learning.

Flexible delivery of learning (B2.3 Technology)

One of the major benefits of e-learning is that it provides new opportunities for the flexible delivery of learning. Online approaches allow learners to work together when separated by both geography and time. Learners can choose when, where and at what speed they study. The growth in portable devices has brought the potential to learn almost anywhere and at any time. This does not mean that successful learning will happen just because a learner has mobile technology or access to the Internet. It requires well-designed learning programmes and materials combined with motivation and appropriate support. It also needs the learners to have the appropriate mix of learning skills, such as managing their time and accepting responsibility for their own learning. A learner without the necessary skills who is required to take part using mobile learning is likely to fail.

Online learning

Online learning is often associated with poor retention rates compared to face-to-face methods. The characteristics of successful online learners have been identified by several writers and researchers. Clarke (2008) summarised them as:

- Confident and previously successful learners
- Motivated
- Having good communication, collaboration and co-operative skills
- Competent users of technology.

An important part of any e-learning programme is helping learners to develop these skills and characteristics. There is little point attracting learners with the benefits of anytime and anywhere learning if a large proportion fails to complete the course successfully. Learners need to be supported in a flexible way to match the nature of the technology.

It can be a challenge for teachers working with distance learners because many methods of assessing who needs help are based on seeing the learner or on their appearance at regular face-to-face sessions. This is missing in a distant relationship that is dependent on communication technologies such as e-mail. The teacher's role is often to facilitate or moderate learning and involves:

- Motivating learners to participate and collaborate with each other
- Carefully monitoring participation in order to identify learners who need support
- Fast reactions to questions (i.e. communication technologies are often associated with immediate responses)
- Systematic checking on learners' progress
- Proactive involvement to achieve objectives.

Community learning

There is a long and successful tradition of taking learning into the community, to reach people who would probably not attend a college or a formal institute. If your previous experiences of education have been poor then your willingness to participate is likely to be low. However, many adults with poor initial educational experiences are often willing to take part in learning that is based near their homes in their own communities.

The challenge for the teacher is not only to raise self-confidence and self-esteem of the learners but also to overcome the barriers of working in a site not designed for teaching. Technology provides the means of making the resources of a purpose-built location available in the community. Portable equipment means that electronic whiteboards, digital cameras and the many other useful devices can be used. It is possible to transport in the boot of a car all that is necessary to create a modern technological classroom almost anywhere. The main limitations are often the lack of an Internet connection, limited numbers of power points and the lack of support staff in outreach locations. The latter implies that the outreach teacher needs more technical skills to avoid small issues becoming blocks to effective teaching.

The ability to connect to the Internet using a mobile phone link and long-life batteries have overcome to some extent these limitations. However, you are always going to need to be self-reliant to some extent and it is important to plan community learning by:

- Visiting the location before the learning programme starts to be aware of the available resources, to check the environment is safe and to consider the layout of the facilities.

- Arriving early for each session to give plenty of time for setting up equipment. This is usually accompanied by later departure to allow for removing equipment and loading cars. Often learners will help with both once trust is established.

- Ensuring you have spares for the equipment such as fuses, plugs and bulbs. Remember you cannot simply go down the corridor to get help.

Community locations, although not purpose-built for learning, are often more flexible in that you can change the layout of the space. You could arrange for people to sit and work in small groups or for everyone to form a circle, whatever fits your approach. Popular locations are nursery and primary schools where the parents of the children are often motivated to attend. Many schools are keen to involve parents. The key to success is often timing so that parents stay at the school to take part in the programme after bringing their children to school or they complete a session in time to take them home. Although schools are often technologically well resourced, there are frequently many practical issues to overcome in order to use them with adults, such as:

- Furniture and layout are designed for small children so may be uncomfortable for adults to use.

- Access to the Internet is controlled to prevent children visiting unsuitable websites and this often severely limits the use by adults.

- The computers and other equipment are being used by the children and may simply not be available.

- After-school use is often determined by the availability of the school ICT technician or caretaker and the payment of overtime can be a significant factor.

You should not assume access, so check with the headteacher to ensure it can be used for your purposes.

Mobile learning

A few minutes of observation on a college campus will reveal that many learners now carry a range of portable devices such as mobile phones, video cameras and MP3 players. These have become increasingly sophisticated with many mobile phones offering their users access to the Internet while on the move, inbuilt video cameras, instant messaging, access to conferencing and many other online services all in a single pocket-sized device. This opens up many possibilities to support learning through mobile devices. However, we should also realise that a mobile environment may include noise, crowded spaces (e.g. on a bus) and a range of other distractions. These factors need to be considered in the design of mobile learning activities. Ones that require concentration over a long time may not be suitable whereas short chunks of learning may be a better fit for learning on the move.

Mobile technology covers many different devices and purposes. They have been used in education and training for numerous roles such as:

- Digital photographs to provide evidence of competency and illustrate assignments
- Speech recording to collect evidence for projects
- Video recording to provide feedback (e.g. sports science)
- Text messaging to remind learners of deadlines
- PDAs to provide flexible, on-the-move access to online resources.

The functionality of mobile devices is increasing continuously meaning that learning possibilities are expanding all the time. It is difficult to generalise but anytime and anywhere learning is rapidly becoming possible. Cochrane (2010) identified a number of success factors in using mobile learning. They showed the importance of selecting the most appropriate equipment and use of it in terms of the nature of the course as well as providing feedback to learners.

PRACTICAL EXAMPLE – IPHONE APPS

The iPhone combines a mobile phone with Internet access, music player and a video camera. There are many apps (i.e. applications) available for the iPhone, many of which are free. You can gain access to blogs, twitter and many websites (e.g. news) directly from your iPhone and can also install apps to turn your phone into a global positioning system (GPS), a library of books and a variety of other things. It therefore has huge potential for learning and fits into a jacket pocket or handbag. The iPad offers very similar benefits plus a larger screen and customisation to view information through the system. It is easily passed around a group so enhancing collaboration.

Mobile technology is often linked to informal learning with users employing it to find information on a just-in-time basis. They use GPS, maps and other resources to navigate to new locations thus helping them improve their knowledge of the geography of the area. While on holiday they can find out the history of an area while recording their personal experiences through digital photographs or short video films. These can be uploaded to websites so that family and friends can see what they are doing. These functions that support informal experiences can be used for more formal learning with defined structures.

> **PRACTICAL EXAMPLE – MOMO (MOBILE MOODLE)**
>
> MOMO is an add-on for Moodle to allow mobile learning – a JAVA-based client for mobile phones allowing them access to learning materials on the move. It is available from www.mobilemoodle.org/.

Mobile technology is now part of most people's lives. A train or bus journey will illustrate this fact with the majority of people texting, making or receiving calls and accessing the Internet through their mobile devices.

PDAs and smart functions

PDAs and smart phones provide a wealth of functions that can be carried in a person's pocket. The inbuilt functions are often supplemented with applications (apps) that can be bought or, in many cases, downloaded for free. There are many thousands of applications available and the number is growing at an astonishing rate. Whilst most applications are not intended for educational use, many can be used for learning. Some possible uses of functions and applications are:

- Using the PDA/smart phone clock as a stop watch or timer to manage time (e.g. project interviews, experiments and surveys)
- Using GPS functions (e.g. in field trips, projects and research)
- Using financial apps (e.g. in accountancy, management and business studies)
- Using news apps (e.g. media studies)
- Using health and dietary apps.

PDAs and smart phones now combine what were separate devices such as music and sound players, cameras and GPS as well as providing access to e-mail and the Internet.

Podcasts (B2.3 Technology)

The availability of portable MP3 players and the development of Really Simple Syndication (RSS) distribution have made possible the large-scale use of podcasts, which are audio recordings to present information about a topic, interviews between experts and other recordings. They can be created relatively easily using open source applications such as Audacity, a microphone and a modern laptop or desktop.

> **PRACTICAL EXAMPLE – AUDACITY**
>
> Audacity is a free, open source sound recording and editing application, widely used to create podcasts. It is available from http://audacity.sourceforge.net/.

Although it is technically straightforward to create a podcast, there is more to effective audio learning than simply the technology. Audio recording needs to engage the listener through well thought out content and a voice that holds the attention of the learner. Not everyone has an effective voice and simply recording what comes to mind is likely to produce an incoherent and rambling podcast. You need to create a script, which can be read from to produce the recording. It should not be too long since listeners are often likely to listen to it while travelling. If the subject is long, then break it down into short sections so that the learner can stop and start the material. It is also useful to begin with a clear explanation of the topic and structure of the material. A summary of the key points is also useful at the end or at regular intervals in a long recording.

Activity 3.12 Podcasting

Write a script for a podcast on a subject that you think will be suitable for recording. Break the script into short segments about four minutes long with an opening explaining the topic and structure of the podcast (e.g. four × four-minute segments with a final conclusion, each separated by an interval of ten seconds).

Record the script using Audacity or another tool and ask a group of students to listen to it and give you feedback on its effectiveness.

Creating an effective podcast is often the challenge that teachers focus on, but it is also critical to ensure that the learners gain from listening the recording. One approach is to encourage them to listen and take notes. Learners can be provided with gapped handouts to encourage them to complete them. The gaps are intended to focus their attention of the key issues. However, Bennett and Reynolds (2009) reporting on their studies of podcasting effectiveness, identified that confident learners found gapped handouts limiting. These learners took notes anyway, using them to help identify the key issues and arrive at their own conclusions. Bennett and Reynolds (2009) concluded that gapped handouts were probably more appropriate with less independent learners.

Bennett and Reynolds (2009) compared the learning effectiveness of podcasting with text-based materials using Bloom's taxonomy (1956). The learning was broadly the same but with podcasts stronger on assisting learners to synthesise and evaluate. This is an interesting outcome and combined with the increased flexibility for learners to choose where and when they learn, shows the potential of the approach.

Learners are going to listen to the podcast in different ways. Some will almost certainly want to listen while travelling but others will listen at home or college using a computer's audio facilities. This is an important point to consider when creating the material. A listener who is moving is unable to take notes so it is poor practice to suggest that they do so. You need to provide material that gives the learners choice of where and how they listen.

Communicating with learners (B3.1 Technology)

There are many different ways of communicating with your learners, including:

- E-mail
- Texting
- Twitter
- VLE discussion forum
- Blog comments
- Instant messaging.

E-mail

It is important initially to distinguish between asynchronous and synchronous communication. The first allows messages to be sent to learners who are not physically present at the time it was sent. They can read it later when it is convenient for them. This is useful if you want to send a message to the whole class. You are not constrained by the need for them all to be available. Thus e-mail, an asynchronous method, is very useful and efficient for messages to multiple recipients. It also has the advantage of attachments, allowing you to send information or materials. Its main limitation is that you do not know when your learners will read the message.

Texting

Texting is also asynchronous but people tend to read and send text messages almost continuously, giving it the potential to be read while people are on the move and thus it is perhaps quicker than e-mail. However, it is a relatively informal communication channel and limited to short messages so most appropriate for communicating reminders about deadlines, unexpected changes to programmes (e.g. cancelled sessions) and other short messages.

Twitter

Twitter is also limited to short messages and is intended for a series of related communications. It is perhaps most suitable for learners to communicate with each other about a joint project or activity rather than being used by the teacher. An exception would be when you are offering group feedback such as explaining a misconception or giving directions.

Discussion forum

Discussion forums are again a group asynchronous communication method. Readers need to go proactively to the forum. In contrast, e-mail is sent to the individual it is addressed to. You cannot be sure when a forum message will be read so it is perhaps not the most effective for urgent news. However, it is a permanent message, remaining on view as long as the forum exists. You need to weigh carefully what you need to say in a forum since it may be difficult to change.

Blog comments

Comments on a learner's blog are obviously intended as feedback to that individual. If the blog is open to other learners then you need to be sensitive about the nature of your communication. The message is a permanent record and you cannot be sure when the learner will read your comments. You should aim at providing supportive and motivating messages that help the learners develop their reflective skills.

Instant messaging

Instant messaging is a synchronous communication method. It allows pairs or small groups to discuss issues through text messages or in some cases audio and video. Its strength is that you can have short discussions while being geographically separated. Its limitation is that everyone needs to be available at the same time and it is not suitable for large groups. In education, you could perhaps offer short revision tutorials for small groups using instant messaging. Alternatively, a virtual classroom can provide synchronous communication using voice, text messaging and shared resources without the limitations on numbers participating.

Activity 3.13 Selecting communication methods

The range of methods discussed in this section provides different ways of communicating with learners. It is important to select the most appropriate means for the specific learners. Consider your own situation. What methods would you select as the most appropriate?

Colleagues (B4.1 Technology)

Electronic individual learning plans

Communication technology supports not only communication with your learners but also with your colleagues. Electronic individual learning plans have the great advantage that they can be shared between staff and learners and can be kept up to date by all the teachers involved with an individual student, allowing everyone to be aware of overall progress. This facilitates the support of the learner by all teachers by keeping them aware of the student's development.

Teachers' discussion forums

VLEs provide not only the means of assisting learners through discussion forums, access to course materials and administration information but also aid teachers through the same resources. Teachers' discussion forums provide them with mutual support that would be difficult to achieve in face-to-face meetings due to teaching commitments, geographical location of venues and other logistical arrangements. Groups of teachers can work together online to develop courses, decide on learning content and moderate assessments. It is an environment for sharing resources and co-operating with each other. Teachers need to maintain and develop their skills and knowledge through CPD. Communication technology offers the means to work with other teachers to develop their expertise jointly.

Sharing resources

Google Docs offers the means to share documents in an environment in which groups of teachers can work together on collaborative projects such as developing policy documents. Sharing offers both synchronous and asynchronous communication so is flexible to meet the needs of most people. Wikis can also provide a means to work collaboratively when producing documents, planning activities and other work.

Learning resources (B5.1 Technology; B4.1 Technology; B2.1 Technology; B2.3 Technology; B1.1 Technology)

There are large volumes of e-learning materials available from many sources. They are sometimes the outcomes of publicly funded projects or from organisations making their learning content available. A worldwide programme (Open Educational Resources), funded by the Hewlett Foundation (http://www.hewlett.org/), has resulted in over a hundred institutions in higher education making materials, in many cases whole courses, available to everyone online. In the UK, the Open University has launched OpenLearn to make its content available. The Learning and Skills Council supported e-learning development for many years as part of the National Learning Network (NLN). This produced a large amount of material in the form of

---

PRACTICAL EXAMPLE – NATIONAL LEARNING NETWORK (NLN) (HTTP://WWW.NLN.AC.UK/)

The NLN was funded by the Learning and Skills Council. It provided substantial funding to produce a large collection of chunks of learning materials for use in the post-compulsory sector. They are available to organisations in the sector and cover adult and community learning, further education, offender learning and skills and work-based learning. Each item of material is designed to provide an interactive learning experience. The NLN materials form the largest collection of learning content for the post-compulsory sector (Figure 3.4).

interactive learning chunks (Figure 3.4). The JISC collections provide access to enormous repositories of digital educational resources. They were mainly developed for higher education but cover a huge area, although JISC repositories are not necessarily open to everyone in the post-compulsory sector.

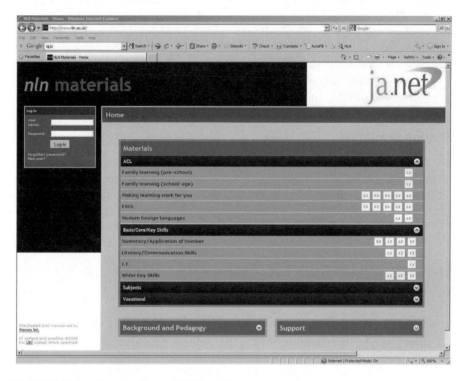

FIGURE 3.4 National Learning Network (NLN) website

PRACTICAL EXAMPLE – OPENLEARN (HTTP://OPENLEARN.OPEN.AC.UK/)

The Open University has provided access to a large volume of its learning materials on the OpenLearn website. These cover many different subjects and are freely available to visitors. The site also provides access to forums, blogs and other resources. It is a major learning resource both to use with learners but also to aid your professional development.

PRACTICAL EXAMPLE – JORUMOPEN (HTTP://OPEN.JORUM.AC.UK/XMLUI/)

This is a repository of Open Educational Resources that have been provided by higher and further education institutions. They are all free to use under a creative commons licence.

PRACTICAL EXAMPLE – GOLD DUST (HTTP://GOLDDUST.BDPLEARNING.COM/)

Gold Dust is a repository of materials aimed at assisting the training and development of teachers. It covers a wide range of issues and includes many different types of materials.

Activity 3.14 Selecting resources

Using the online repositories, select some learning materials to assist your teaching. Consider the objectives that you want the materials to satisfy and choose them in consultation with some of your learners. Reflect on the process you have adopted and contemplate how you would improve it.

Types of resource

A variety of approaches to learning are designed into the various resources that you can obtain. Some of them are:

- Drill and practice activities – these provide some information or instruction followed by the opportunity for the learner to practise, with the system providing feedback on how successful the learner's practice was. The cycle is then repeated with the intention that the learner is given several opportunities to master the information or instruction. This approach has been used extensively for small distinct tasks such as numeracy.

- Simulation – this involves the simulation of a system (e.g. controlling a power plant) or situation (e.g. business) with the learner asked to undertake a task that would normally be difficult in a classroom, either because it is dangerous or too complex. The system provides help and assistance so that the learners get continuous feedback.

- Guided tour – in this type of material learners are guided through a resource such as a virtual laboratory with the key features explained to them. The learners are given choices so that they can have extra explanations of objects that interest them.

The most effective resources are often those that engage the learners by encouraging them to be active. Simple tutorials that give learners facts are often the least useful.

Evaluation of learning resources

With the large volume of learning content that is freely available, it is essential that you are able to evaluate the material to determine its suitability. Clarke (2001a) provides a checklist for evaluating learning materials. The list covers three main areas:

1. Learning issues (e.g. What learning objectives are the materials aiming to support? Who are the target learners?)

2. Presentation/quality of the content (e.g. How do you navigate the content?)

3. Technical issues – hardware and software (e.g. What systems do you need to access the content?).

There are clearly some basic issues to consider in any learning material such as:

- Is the material suitable for the learners (e.g. material designed for children is probably not appropriate for an adult group)?
- Does the material reflect cultural diversity?
- Is the material free of gender stereotyping?
- Is the material accessible?

You have little choice after having checked on the learning content but to test it with your learners. You obviously want to avoid wasting their time so you may simply ask a small group to help. To maximise the use of the learners' time it is worth carefully planning your evaluation. Decide what you want the learners to consider – simply asking them if they liked it will not help you decide whether it is worth including in your course. Consider developing a series of questions to ask the users such as:

1. What did you learn?
2. What did you find most useful?
3. What did you find least useful?
4. If we included the material in the course what could it replace, enhance or extend?

A simple set of questions can be helpful in forming a judgement about the suitability of content but you may also want to observe the learners using the material and interview them to follow up on their answers.

An expert review of the content could be carried out by either another teacher of the same subject or yourself. Again, you need to decide what are the criteria for judging the material, such as:

1. What is the learning objective of the content?
2. Who is the material suitable for?
3. How easy is the material to use?
4. Would your learners accept the learning approach?
5. How is the learning assessed?

A key issue when using any learning content is its copyright. This governs its use, adaptation and development. You should always check the copyright of any content you intend to use. Some will be controlled by a licence for which your institution will have paid while other material will have a Creative Commons licence that allows some degree of development of the material.

PRACTICAL EXAMPLE – CREATIVE COMMONS LICENCE

Creative Commons (http://creativecommons.org/) is an organisation that attempts to make materials freely available so that they can be adapted and developed for the benefit of others. They carry out this aim by providing copyright licences that allow creators to make their work available. The licences are straightforward and make it clear what you are able to do with the materials.

Creating learning materials

There is a wide range of computer applications that can be used by both teachers and learners to create learning materials. Teachers have always developed content to help their learners understand their subjects but technology provides many new tools to create interactive and engaging materials. Many standard applications such as word processors, spreadsheets and presentation systems have been used to produce content. In addition, a wide range of tools has been developed with the focus on developing learning materials (e.g. Hot Potatoes). Several of these tools are open source and freely available. Chapter 4 considers learners developing learning materials in order to engage their interest in their subjects and extend their understanding. This section will concentrate on teachers producing learning content.

Learning materials come in a wide range of shapes and forms. You may simply want to produce better quality handouts. The appearance of a handout is important to engaging the learner in reading and studying its content. A document with spelling and grammatical errors, with a poor layout or containing factual mistakes is not going to motivate readers. Electronic documents allow you to check spelling and grammar or amend them quickly and effectively. In addition, they are easy to communicate as e-mail attachments or to place in a VLE for learners to download. Handouts can be customised for specific groups. For example, there are design guidelines available for dyslexic learners. The Davis Dyslexia Association International (2010) website offers a series of guidelines for website design such as:

- Allow the user to select the font and character size in which to read the information
- Use short paragraphs
- Maximise the contrast between foreground and background.

PRACTICAL EXAMPLE – HOT POTATOES (HTTP://HOTPOT.UVIC.CA/)

Hot Potatoes is a group of applications aimed at creating educational materials for different types of assessment, including self-assessment. The applications are freeware.

Some examples of the possibilities offered by applications include:

- Microsoft PowerPoint – adding multimedia, hyperlinks and interactivity to a presentation
- Microsoft Word – creating check boxes to help you develop multiple-choice activities
- Microsoft Excel – creating a model for the learner to explore by adding data
- Google Forms – developing an online survey or questionnaire
- Xerte – a tool to help you create interactive browser-based learning materials
- eLearning XHTML Editor – an open source authoring tool that aims to assist you develop learning materials
- Wink – a tool for creating learning materials through screen captures and thus mostly aimed at learning about software and applications.

Images

It is said that a picture is worth a thousand words. It is probably impossible to prove but illustrations and images do add considerable interest to documents. There are many ways of producing images but one simple and effective way is to capture the image that appears on a screen. There are lots of tools available to do this, for example the Windows Vista snipping tool. The captured images can be inserted into applications such as Microsoft Word, Excel, Publisher and PowerPoint. They can then be edited using a range of applications, the most straightforward probably being Windows Paint, which is a Windows accessory.

Digital cameras are very useful tools for capturing experiences such as group or individual projects. Microsoft PhotoStory is an application that allows a series of images to be linked with an audio narrative. This enables learners to create a multimedia report on their experiences which is often more interesting and motivating than a written report. These types of interactive story can be used with other groups of learners to provide ideas for future work.

Activity 3.15 Screen capture

Use a screen capture tool to capture an image, edit it and then insert the image into an application. For example, Figure 3.5 shows an image captured with the Windows snipping tool and then edited using Windows Paint.

Design guidance

There are many tools and applications that you can use to create learning materials making it a relatively straightforward task. However, good design is not achieved by accident, but rather through the adoption of sound principles. Some basic principles are:

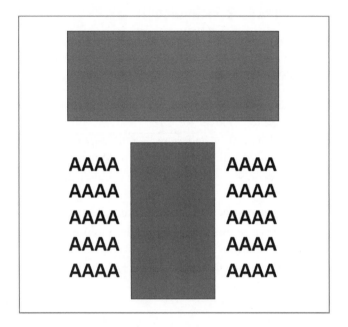

FIGURE 3.5 Screen capture using rectangle function in Windows snipping tool

- Agree the aims and objectives that you want the materials to meet.
- Involve your learners in the design process. Their viewpoint will not be the same as your own. Materials need to be accepted by the learners so that they are motivated to use them.
- Create a plan, outline design or storyboard for your materials.
- Avoid the over-use of colour, font and character sizes and other visual options. They can distract from the contents. Use the various options for distinct purposes such as emphasising key points or separating different sections of content.
- Provide controls and navigation that are clearly visible to the users.
- Be consistent so that learners know where to look and what to do.
- Undertake a small scale trial to test the material before using widely with learners.
- Evaluate your content with learners.

The design of learning materials requires skill and understanding of both the subject and design. Clarke (2001b) explains that designing learning materials is a complex task involving blending various factors together. Clark and Mayer (2003) provide considerable assistance to developers by offering guidelines for creating multimedia materials.

Supporting learners (B5.2 Technology)

It is not enough to provide learners with learning materials, tools and applications and expect them to be successful. You need to provide them with appropriate support. Some useful actions to take to support learners are:

- Introduce them to e-learning at an early stage of the course so that they are aware of what to expect.
- Provide them with a clear understanding of the purpose of using e-learning (e.g. capturing evidence for their competency portfolios).
- Make clear the aims and objectives they should achieve through using the e-learning content.
- Provide briefing documents explaining what they have to do and why.
- Encourage mutual support (i.e. learners are often more willing to ask peers for help than a teacher).
- Develop guides to the use of applications and tools.

Personal issues

The final activity involves returning to Activity 3.1 and considering how technology can aid your personal learning and teaching objectives.

Activity 3.16 Recap of Activity 3.1

In Activity 3.1 you created a list of the main issues you would like to improve. Now try to identify e-learning approaches that might help you address these points. For example:

1. Improve motivation and interest of learners in the subject – add more group activities such as webquests, creating a podcast or developing a presentation using video cameras/electronic whiteboard.
2. Encourage more peer support outside the classroom – create a learners' e-mail discussion group and provide encouragement to use it for asking and answering questions as well as discussing issues. You might link some or all of the group activities to it.
3. Improve personal presentation methods – word process handouts, use presentation software and create interactive materials.
4. Achieve better outcomes – seek ways of providing formative feedback through methods such as annotating assignments, providing comments on learners' diaries (e.g. blogs) and encouraging peer assessment.

Summary

The main points of this chapter are:

- In order to identify the most appropriate e-learning methods to use, it is critical to consider your learning and teaching objectives.

- Learning environments that motivate learners and are not limited by the physical limitations of the classroom or time can be created in several ways through the application of technology.

- Many education providers in the post-compulsory sector have implemented a VLE. VLEs offer a range of functions such as downloadable resources, access to course information, discussion forums, online libraries, blogs and wikis.

- Discussion groups require a support environment and real reasons to participate in order to be successful. This can take several weeks to establish.

- Forums offer many advantages such as everyone being free to contribute without restraint, a permanent record of contributions so that the whole discussion can be considered and time to consider contributions to encourage more in-depth discussions.

- Forums do have limitations such as some learners being reluctant to contribute and needing encouragement. It is easy to misunderstand messages so it is important that everyone follows the rules of participation (i.e. netiquette).

- Virtual classrooms are now available that offer a range of functions such as a shared whiteboard, video and audio conferencing, text, audio and video communications, sharing a computer desktop and quizzes. They are employed for online conferences, tutorials, seminars, staff training and presentations.

- Many people use social networks for personal reasons but this does not mean they understand how to employ them as part of their education and training.

- Wikis allow groups of learners to collaborate to create a joint document.

- Appropriate support is critical to the success of all online learning environments.

- It is critical that learners are able to recognise the benefits of taking part in online learning environments.

- From the many different e-learning approaches you need to select the ones that are most likely to meet the learners' needs and your objectives.

- You have a responsibility to ensure the safety of your learners. Sharples et al. (2008) in a report for Becta stated that 'Safe internet use requires balancing perceived benefits against acceptable risks.'

- To become an independent learner requires both technical and learning skills.

- Feedback is important to the development of independence.

- E-learning provides for the flexible delivery of learning so that learners can choose when, where and at what speed to study.

- Technology can assist community teachers to improve their learners' self-confidence and self-esteem.

- Many learners own and carry a range of sophisticated portable devices. They offer the opportunity to support learning while on the move but it is important when designing exercises that we realise that the mobile environment may be noisy, crowded and distracting.

- Podcasts can potentially be used on a large scale due to the availability of MP3 players and the development of RSS distribution.

- There are many ways of communicating with learners and you need to select the most appropriate ones for your learners and context.

- E-learning materials are readily available on the Internet from sources such as the NLN and Open Educational Resources funded by the Hewlett Foundation.

- It is essential that you are able to evaluate e-learning material to decide if it is suitable (i.e. for your learners, subject and quality).

- Interactive and engaging learning materials can also be created by both teachers and learners using both standard applications (e.g. word processors) and specialist tools (e.g. Hot Potatoes).

- Successful learning materials require good design assisted by the use of sound principles.

Specialist Learning and Teaching

Teaching standards (LLUK, 2007)

The standard statements CS1 to CS4 with the associated technology elements C1.1 to C4.1 Technology are covered in this chapter that deals with how technology impacts in your own teaching area. There are clear links between the contents of this chapter and Chapter 3.

Introduction

While e-learning has been successfully employed across a wide range of subjects, some approaches will be more appropriate to your own area than others. You need to decide which are likely to be most applicable and will gain the best results. The post-compulsory education sector covers a very wide range of contexts and subjects. In some areas, the availability of computers and broadband connections are very limited. In a prison, for example, there are limitations on the types of technology that are permitted so that the context of the education and training constrains your choice. In community-based provision, the equipment often needs to be transported to the location so limiting both the range of technology available and the connectivity. Portability is a key factor in community-based courses. There are many examples of digital cameras being employed successfully to provide a focus for group work, capture evidence of competency for portfolio assessment and create learning materials in adult and community learning.

Even in locations with adequate technological resources you will probably have to make choices. If you need to give every learner access to a personal computer, you may have to use technology in classrooms that are poorly laid out for group interaction. Many rooms designed for ICT classes have computers around and facing the wall. This does not encourage peer support and may influence your choice of e-learning methods to employ.

Your subject will have its own characteristics and you will need to decide what technology and approaches will be most useful. A good deal of evidence exists that shows many learners with poor literacy skills are motivated to learn through and with the use of ICT. Word processing provides an obvious approach in that learners are able to write with the support of a spelling and grammar checker, in addition to their being able to edit their own writing. A subject that includes developing group collaboration skills might benefit from using a wiki, which often supports group working. Equally, the need to develop reflective skills might be aided by the use of blogs for reflective writing and discussion. Developing a podcast might be helpful, not only in researching the content but also in developing speaking skills.

Maintaining and developing your expertise (C4.1 Technology; C1.2 Technology)

In a fast-moving world, it is vital to maintain your own expertise and subject understanding. CPD is now a requirement of maintaining your Qualified Teacher status. E-learning is in continuous development and growth so if you want to sustain your knowledge and skills, you need to focus on your professional development as a normal part of your work. Although this sounds a formidable task, technology can assist the process in many ways.

Searching for information

Probably the most obvious use of technology in maintaining and developing your understanding and knowledge is through the use of the World Wide Web as a source of information. Researching the contents of websites will allow you to:

- Identify resources for your teaching
- Identify opportunities to develop your knowledge and skills in your specialist area (e.g. conferences, webinars and development events)
- Locate examples and case studies demonstrating how to use e-learning in your subject
- Find podcasts to update your subject knowledge.

The general search engines, although extremely powerful and useful, normally do not search what is called the deep web. The deep web is those parts of the web that are dynamic and far more extensive than the websites that we normally read. The deep web includes databases, images, restricted/protected content that can only be accessed using a password, information not presented as webpages, blog contents, social network discussions and similar material.

Specialist search engines have been designed to concentrate on searching the deep web and locate specific types of information. Many are focused on particular subjects and are particularly useful in locating resources to assist your professional development. General search engines such as Google can often be used to locate the specialist engine. Google also offers help to keep yourself informed of new development through Google Alerts.

PRACTICAL EXAMPLE – EXAMPLES OF SPECIALIST SEARCH ENGINES

Some examples of search engines that you can use to locate books are:

1. Google Books – http://books.google.co.uk/
2. Abebooks – second-hand books held by thousands of dealers – http://www.abebooks.com/
3. Bookfinder – http://www.bookfinder.com/
4. BibliOZ – out of print books – http://www.biblioz.com/
5. AddALL – http://www.addall.com/.

PRACTICAL EXAMPLE – GOOGLE ALERTS

Google offers a specialist service to make you aware of news and new developments in a subject of your choice. The updates are e-mailed to you and you can use the links contained in the e-mail to follow up particular items. You can have as many alerts as you wish. The alerts are available at http://www.google.com/alerts?hl=en&gl=.

The following practical example demonstrates the specialist collection offered by the Excellence Gateway website for the post-compulsory education sector. This is a large resource of information for anyone teaching in the sector.

PRACTICAL EXAMPLE – EXCELLENCE GATEWAY COMMUNITY

The Excellence Gateway (http://www.excellencegateway.org.uk/) is a huge online resource for people working in the post-compulsory education sector. It provides access to a large amount of information to assist teachers in all subjects.

The Excellence Gateway Community offers the means to meet and collaborate with other people working in the sector through general, specific and collaborative forums and online workshops. You can join existing groups or start your own. This is a useful means of maintaining and extending your understanding of your subject and teaching.

PRACTICAL EXAMPLE – VIRTUAL TRAINING SUITE

The Virtual Training Suite was developed for learners in higher education who needed to improve their research and search skills in the context of specific subjects. It covers a wide range of subjects and is available at http://www.vts.intute.ac.uk/. It is currently a free service but this may change in the future.

Online journals

There has recently been a large increase in the availability of online journals covering almost every subject. Some journals are available in both print and online forms but many are only available online. Some are free while others require a subscription to gain access. Many colleges and universities subscribe to a range of online journals. In addition to simply providing papers on a range of subjects, journals often provide a searchable archive of all papers they have been published, blogs from experts and the means for readers to add comments. Journals are both a resource for researching your subject and also a means of gaining insight into teaching methods.

Activity 4.1 Search for suitable journals

Use search engines of your own choice to locate a range of journals that is appropriate to your subject. Subscribe to ones that you feel will help you maintain and develop your professional knowledge.

E-newsletters

Many professional bodies and organisations offer e-newsletters for members or, in some cases, anyone who is willing to register. The JISC offers a range of newsletters covering the various aspects of their technological developments (e.g. collections of digital resources). Individual Regional Support Centres also provide e-newsletters covering different aspects of their e-learning work. The Chartered Institute for Personnel and Development provides a weekly e-newsletter for registered site users.

Newsletters are sent to you automatically once you have registered so you can keep up to date relatively easily. The newsletters are often linked to other resources so that they provide more information than the printed form.

Activity 4.2 Search for a suitable e-newsletter

Use search engines of your own choice to locate a range of e-newsletters that is appropriate to your subject. Subscribe to the ones that you feel will help you maintain and develop your professional knowledge.

Specialist discussion groups

Another useful way to help maintain and extend your professional understanding of your subject and related areas is to use online discussion forums. There is a very large number of forums and many organisations (e.g. Excellence Gateway) provide ones that cover specific subjects. You can again use general and specialist search engines to locate forums that are most useful to you. In some cases, organisations provide the means for individuals to start their own and Activity 4.3 offers you the opportunity to create one.

Activity 4.3 Excellence Gateway community collaborative workrooms

Use the collaborative workrooms facilities in the Excellence Gateway (http://www. excellencegateway.org.uk/) to establish an online forum for your colleagues, team or department to meet to discuss issues.

Alternatively review the existing general and specific forums to locate ones that are suitable to maintain and extend your subject knowledge and skills.

Online resources

Chapter 3 discussed the availability of online collections of learning materials. These are often a useful resource, demonstrating how other teachers have approached the delivery of particular aspects of your subject. Many universities provide podcasts on specialist subjects, which may well offer you the means of professional development. These can be located using a search engine, but iTunes has a collection of over 100,000 podcasts covering a very wide range. Many will not be specifically useful but it is a resource worth exploring. The iTunes search facility (www.apple.com/uk/iTunes) will locate podcasts that interest you.

RSS feeds automatically distribute content such as podcasts and other types of material, so once you have located a source that provides an RSS feed, you can be kept up to date without any extra effort. You do need to subscribe and install a reader.

Activity 4.4 Podcasts and other material for professional development

Search the World Wide Web for podcasts and other material including the iTunes collection of podcasts to locate content that will be useful to help your professional development.

Good practice

Help with various forms of good practice, including within teaching, is often made available online for ease of access and distribution. The Excellence Gateway is specifically aimed at improving the quality of the post-compulsory education sector. The site is also home to the Ofsted database of good practice. Ofsted is aiming to illustrate the best practice in teaching and learning in the sector.

PRACTICAL EXAMPLE – EXCELLENCE GATEWAY

The Excellence Gateway provides a large collection of e-learning case studies with the aim of improving teaching and learning. They are available at http://www.excellencegateway.org.uk/page.aspx?o=case-studies-teaching-and-learning.

PRACTICAL EXAMPLE – OFSTED GOOD PRACTICE DATABASE

The Excellence Gateway also provides access to the Ofsted Good Practice Database. It is available at http://www.excellencegateway.org.uk/page.aspx?o=goodpracticedatabase.

CPD records (C1.2 Technology)

As you will have realised, technology can play an important role in helping you maintain and extend your specialist knowledge and skills and gain more understanding of e-learning. However, we have not considered technological approaches to managing and recording your professional activities.

The Institute for Learning provides Reflect, an online e-portfolio for teachers in the post-compulsory education sector to record their CPD.

PRACTICAL EXAMPLE – INSTITUTE FOR LEARNING'S REFLECT PORTFOLIO

Reflect is the online portfolio for members of the Institute for Learning, providing the means to manage and record your development activities. Using an application on your iPhone or iPod Touch, you can record and reflect on your experiences while on the move. The Institute supports the use of Reflect.

An e-portfolio can not only provide you with a means of recording activities but it can also help you plan your professional development, reflect on your experiences in order to gain the most from them and identify gaps or further activities that are needed. An e-portfolio offers you a range of functions that can help you maintain and extend your skills such as:

- Competency frameworks to compare yourself against
- Skills audits to help you identify your needs
- A learning journal to help you reflect on your experiences as a teacher and consider your understanding of your subject
- Tools to present your experience, skills and knowledge
- Planning applications.

Professional e-portfolios are not a short-term device but rather a long-term process to help you manage your professional life. You need to consider how to transfer the information they contain as your career and life changes. The information will grow in value so that after a few years e-portfolios will not be replaceable. You should aim to keep a backup copy and you may want to decide on storage in the clouds, i.e. online, your own computer or elsewhere.

What e-learning tools and techniques are available? (C1.2 Technology)

There is a bewildering range of e-learning tools and techniques that may be appropriate to your teaching subject. The challenge is to be aware of the possibilities and be able to decide which ones to use. The most complex and demanding will not necessarily gain you the best results; it may be the most straightforward one. You need to use your specialist understanding and skills to decide what is most appropriate for you and your learners.

You may want consider the role the tools or techniques are going to play in your teaching and learning, for example:

- Digital camera – to capture evidence for a competency-based assessment (e.g. cutting a hole in a wall using a hammer and chisel)
- Video camera – to help you provide feedback on a learner's manual skill or performance (e.g. yoga class)
- Blogging – to assist learners develop reflection
- Online submission of assignments – this is often helpful to part-time learners who will not need to make a special journey to submit their work.

Using the Kolb experiential learning cycle

One approach when considering the role of technology is to employ the Kolb (1984) experiential learning cycle. Figure 4.1 shows a cycle based on Kolb (1984) showing four steps in a learning cycle. You could analyse tools and techniques against the cycle to identify how you could employ them. In many cases a tool can serve several purposes depending on how you use it.

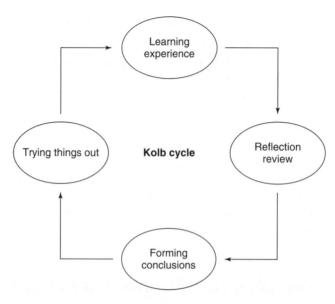

FIGURE 4.1 Kolb cycle (1984)

Stage 1: Learning experience – this covers the leaner's classroom experience so includes tools that can aid the presentation of information, those that would aid carrying out tasks and those of assessment.

Stage 2: Reflection and review of the learning experience – this includes blogs, and twitter that help learners reflect on their experiences.

Stage 3: Forming conclusions – this may include a range of tools depending on the type of learning experience, for example, mind mapping applications.

Stage 4: Trying things out – essentially applying the conclusions the learner has come to following reflection on the learning experience. This may include a wide range of technology depending on the context, such as a stop watch on a mobile phone.

Activity 4.5 Selecting tools

Consider your own specialist subject and select one aspect that you would like to improve through using technology. Use the Kolb cycle to consider what tools you could employ.

PRACTICAL EXAMPLE – ICT BASICS

There are many resources to help learners practise the basic ICT skills (learning experience) such as:

1. Computer user tutorial – www.bbc.co.uk/webwise
2. Mousercise beginners' tutorial – http://latebloomers.us/mousercise/index.htm
3. Mouse skills – http://www.pbclibrary.org/mousing/games.htm.

PRACTICAL EXAMPLE – HAND-HELD VIDEO CAMERA

Hand-held video cameras have been used in a range of settings to motivate small groups to illustrate projects with short videos. For example, a group of English for speakers of other languages (ESOL) learners investigating public transport.

PRACTICAL EXAMPLE – GROUP WORKING

Many employers will be seeking individuals who can work in teams. Wikis provide a natural tool to encourage group working and collaboration through communication.

Evaluation of your own use of technology

It is important to evaluate and review the use of technology in your teaching. You should reflect on how it has impacted on your work in both positive and negative ways. One approach to reflection is to:

1. Record your observations of the experience – this will often help you remember all the details.

2. Analyse the experience in a systematic and critical way, considering the strengths and weaknesses of your approach.

3. Consider your context as this often has a large effect on an approach, and reflect on what influenced it has had.

4. Consider what improvements you could make in using the approach.

In combination with your own reflections, involve your learners in the evaluation. There is a range of ways of undertaking a user review. Encourage them to reflect on their experiences. It is often helpful if you want to focus on a specific approach to provide them with a framework for their analysis. This could be an electronic form, created using the Form application in Google Docs or something similar. This has the advantage that the results are presented in a spreadsheet, which will make subsequent consideration easier.

Presentation (C2.1 Technology)

In most subjects there are occasions when an issue or topic needs to be presented to a group of learners. The blackboard was one of the first tools provided in the classroom to assist the presentation of information and to record the outcomes of discussion and interaction. It is interesting to note that this took several decades to become an established approach. New technology has provided many tools to aid the presentation of information and to assist the interaction between the teacher, learner and subject. It is important, however, to realise that simply using them to present information employs merely a small proportion of their potential. Their true power lies in engaging and motivating learners to participate. Cox et al. (2003) in a review of research evidence concluded that attainment was improved when learners were encouraged to discuss and contest their understanding individually, in small groups or as a whole class. The review focused on children's education but the outcomes are still appropriate to older learners.

All presentation technology can be used by both learners and teachers. In many cases, in-depth learning is more likely to result if the learners are actively involved in using the technology.

Interactive whiteboard

Interactive whiteboards have been employed extensively across the different education sectors and are in use with all ages of learners. They have many benefits such as:

- They are a multimedia device and can be used with a range of input devices.
- They can be employed with text, graphics, still images, sound and video.
- They can be used with a whole class, a small group or an individual.
- They can be used by either learners, teachers or in combination.
- Material can be prepared in advance and stored electronically to be used many times.
- Prepared content can be annotated and extended during a session with the results stored for future use.
- Groups can share their understanding with the whole class.

There are various ways of using an interactive whiteboard, but one approach to a large focused session is:

Step 1. Use an ice breaker to engage the learners in the topic that you are going to consider.

Step 2. Brief the group about the tasks and topic.

Step 3. Divide the large group into smaller units that have a specific task to undertake.

Step 4. Get the small groups to report back in plenary, using the interactive whiteboard.

Interactive whiteboards can be combined with other applications to gain the benefits of a powerful presentation tool and the application. Mind mapping software could be used to generate a whole-class analysis of a topic with the results captured by the board and made available to whole group. Office applications (e.g. word processing and spreadsheets) can be used to develop an outline for a project or to analyse or demonstrate mathematical issues. Devices that can be used with a computer, such as an electronic microscope, can be linked to an interactive whiteboard thus allowing the images to be shared with a larger group rather than limiting them to individual work. Presentation, discussion, activities and feedback can be integrated together.

Activity 4.6 Using an interactive whiteboard

It is important to become a confident user of interactive whiteboards. You should not attempt to use them for multiple purposes immediately but rather develop your use over a period. Explore the board to identify its main functions and decide on a specific use. Prepare to use it and try the approach. Learn from the experience and continue the process until you become confident. Do not exclude uses that involve the learners, since this is often very effective and you can learn from your learners' approaches.

Video projectors

Video projectors have been available for several decades but originally they were very large and expensive. Modern projectors are portable with many able to fit into small bags so they can be transported to community or workplace locations. The combination of a laptop computer and projector provides a portable teaching system that enables many locations to be turned into a classroom.

Although projectors have improved in quality, they often need to be used in rooms in which ambient light can be controlled, otherwise the display can be difficult to see. Also, in common with many other projection devices, it is important that you check the whole group can see the display. It is always good practice to view your display from all angles and from both the front and back of the room.

Visualisers

Visualisers are devices that magnify the image of an object placed under a video camera. They are powerful attention directors and are often best used in a spontaneous way to show learners the details of an object too small for them to see clearly in a classroom. They can be used in a wide range of subjects such as:

- Engineering to demonstrate tools, manufactured items, small details on a larger object or generally to add a visual impact to a presentation
- Biology to show details of plants and animals.

Visualisers can be used by both teachers and learners. They are often effective when combined with passing the objects around the group so that learners can handle them and look for the details they have been shown. Visualisers can motivate a group to consider specific issues, such as how an object was manufactured, the purpose of a feature on a plant or how an electrical circuit works. Almost any issue can be illustrated.

PRACTICAL EXAMPLE – PAPERSHOW

Papershow is electronic paper that allows you to carry out interactive presentations, including being able to record learners' comments in a workshop. It is very useful in a variety of settings, including community locations or in the workplace. It is very flexible and easy to transport.

Voting systems

Voting systems are normally combined with a video projector or interactive whiteboard. Excellent at motivating and engaging learners in a topic, they work by asking a group to vote, using hand-held devices, on a series of questions about a subject and then showing the results of the whole group (e.g. a bar chart) on a large screen or interactive whiteboard. They can be used in several ways. Discussion, for example, can be encouraged by asking the group members to explain why they voted in a particular way. As voting systems can be used in any subject, the responses to the questions provide you with opportunities to reinforce points and to assess strengths and weaknesses, as well as allowing you to plan future activities.

Capturing a face-to-face session (C2.1 Technology; C4.1 Technology)

Capturing a face-to-face teaching session on a video so that it can be used later for revision or for other groups is clearly possible. However, there are a number of issues that make it quite challenging to undertake within the law. Two of these are:

- Copyright
- Performing rights.

As an employee, your contract would normally give the copyright of any item created by you as part of your job to your employer. However, it is not entirely clear whether the same is true of learners who may be captured or recorded asking a question. Do you have their permission to film them and later show the result? Then there are performing rights that may allow you to object to a video showing your teaching being shown. In addition, there are probably issues around the Disability Discrimination Act, libel, data protection and things such as capturing a copyrighted item on film.

Technology may allow you to undertake a task that looks useful but there are lots of other issues that need to be considered. Before you attempt filming or allowing a learner to film, please take advice from your employer.

Capturing a face-to-face session can be useful in a variety of ways, such as:

- Another opportunity to understand complex/difficult issues
- Helping learners who speak English as a second language
- Assisting learners with hearing or other impairments
- Increasing flexibility of delivery for learners who have family or care responsibilities.

However, there are other issues that are not so positive such as:

- Learners cannot ask questions of a video
- Interaction between teacher and learners or learner and learner is missing unless they watch the video together
- Learners' study skills may need to change (e.g. more emphasis on taking notes, review and revision skills need to be improved).

It is also useful to consider creating a video that is aimed at revision and that summarises the key points or concentrates on difficult issues. This could be quite short compared to the face-to-face session.

The Australian Learning and Teaching Council reviewed the use of lecture capture (Gosper et al., 2008) in universities and reported an interesting difference in views between staff and students. Generally students were more positive about its use than staff. Students and staff both appreciated the benefits to learners who could not attend the face-to-face session but staff were concerned that some students chose to use the recording rather than the live event. Students said they used the recording in order to take a full set of notes, revise and review material, increase convenience, learn at their own pace and view issues they missed in the session.

JISC Legal offer guidance on the recording of lectures that is available at http://www.jisclegal.ac.uk/ManageContent/ViewDetail/tabid/243/ID/1608/Recording-Lectures-Legal-Considerations-28072010.aspx.

PRACTICAL EXAMPLE – VIDEO

The provision of video presentations in place of a lecture so that learners can study them before attending a face-to-face session has been tried in several institutions. The time used for presentation can be employed for group interaction, questions, discussion and other activities. In this way value is added to the face-to-face session, although this does assume that the main purpose of the session was to impart information.

Using technology to motivate learners (C2.1 Technology)

Technology gives learners the opportunity to be actively involved in their own learning. They can be creative within their chosen subject rather than passive recipients of learning, which can often be ineffective and uninteresting. The employment of technology provides opportunities for learners to demonstrate their skills and knowledge as well as gaining new skills and extending their understanding into new areas. The Web 2.0 technologies have been strongly linked to turning the World Wide Web from the read-only web into the read and write web showing that individuals can play an important part in creating the web's knowledge. The Web 2.0 tools provide the means to create materials and information in a variety of ways.

There are many ways that learners can actively participate in using technology creatively to enhance their learning and, in some cases, assist other learners. Some straightforward examples are:

- Using an electronic whiteboard to explain concepts and ideas or to report on an assignment

- Creating a presentation to show the outcomes of a project

- Taking digital photographs as evidence of competency (e.g. photographs of floral displays shows skill and also provide a resource of ideas for future learners, which, over time, will become a large collection of examples)

- Developing a joint report, with each learner using a wiki to add and edit content

- Producing an online survey to investigate attitudes to an aspect of the subject they are studying.

Technology can be used creatively within any subject to excite and motivate learners.

Making learning fun

A fun tool to use is Wordle (http://www.wordle.net/), which allows you to create an image based on the frequency of words within a document. This is called a word cloud. Figure 4.2 shows a Wordle picture based on an analysis of an earlier section of this book. The process of creating an image can be a motivating experience in that it provides a focus for group discussion, a means of analysing a document such as learners' assignments or a group project and it produces a summary of issues in a new and novel way. Wordle can bring a subject alive for learners as it presents it from a different viewpoint.

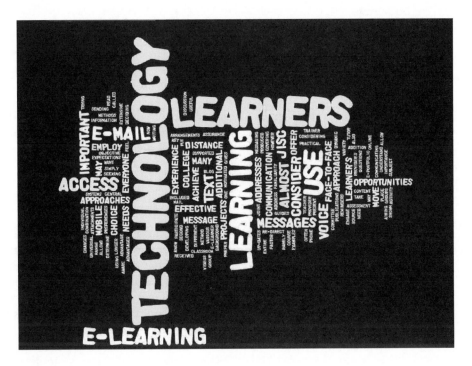

FIGURE 4.2 Wordle example

Digital storytelling

Digital storytelling is a powerful and exciting method that encourages and develops creativity. Technology is used to enhance and present stories in a new and interesting format such as through the use of video cameras, audio recording and other tools. It is motivating way to gain the attention and active involvement of learners who might not be interested in writing a report or undertaking a conventional assignment. An educational digital story is normally short (i.e. two to ten minutes) and uses a variety of tools depending on the learners. It might employ Microsoft Photostory, a free application that allows you to blend still images with a narrative to present a story or perhaps use a video with Microsoft PowerPoint. The choice is yours and the learners in deciding what is appropriate. Hand-held cameras that can take video and download it to a computer are widely available. They enable a narrator to provide a voice-over as the film is made. Hand-held sound recorders are also available, as are digital cameras.

Digital storytelling can be used in any subject and has been used extensively by individuals to recount their personal stories. In education they could be employed to:

- Present the technology needs of an organisation
- Describe an engineering project

- Assist ESOL students develop their speaking skills
- Help hairdressing students demonstrate their skills
- Create evidence for a CV in performing arts
- Demonstrate learners' understanding of health and safety.

Digital storytelling can be applied to any subject or course. It is exciting and highly motivating to many learners. Digital storytelling provides a focus for an assignment or project. It allows learners to work together and therefore develop team working skills that are often prized by many employers.

Creating learning materials

The involvement of learners in practical projects to develop an outcome has been widely used in all aspects of education and training. Individual or group activity is a common feature of probably all subjects. Technology provides a rich range of tools and applications to enhance the approach and allow learners to undertake work that previously was impossible or impracticable. One focus is to give learners the objective of creating learning materials for their own course and subject. This has many benefits but those that stand out are:

1. The creators have to analyse the subject systematically in order to develop the materials and thus they become experts in that aspect of the subject.
2. In order to produce learning materials for other learners, the developers need to gain a clear understanding of the problems other learners may encounter in understanding the content. This will help them develop their own understanding.
3. The developers will need to consider alternative approaches to presenting the learning and thus need to explore the subject from different viewpoints.
4. The team will need to support each other through sharing skills and understanding.
5. The developers will need to explore how to work together as a team.
6. The learners will have opportunities to extend their technical skills and knowledge.
7. Other learners in the course will gain from sharing the resources created.
8. Future learners will benefit from accessing the created resources.

Many applications have been specifically developed to create learning materials. Many tools are freely available.

Microsoft PowerPoint has been used extensively by both teachers and learners to produce content. It has the advantage of being widely available and can blend together graphics, video, audio and text into engaging packages.

Often the most straightforward approaches are the most effective. Learners equipped with hand-held video cameras can often capture many examples relevant to their studies (e.g. practical skills – cutting a pipe, laying a brick and planting seeds).

These examples help learners by providing interest and motivation but also assist others with numerous examples of practice to demonstrate how tasks can be carried out. Over a period of time you will create a large archive of materials.

PRACTICAL EXAMPLE – eXe

eXe is an open source authoring tool to help you create learning materials. It is available from http://exelearning.org/. Visit the website and gain an understanding of the possibilities for developing learning materials.

PRACTICAL EXAMPLE – XERTE

Xerte is a tool to help you create interactive browser-based learning materials. It is available from http://www.nottingham.ac.uk/xerte/toolkits.htm. Visit the website and gain an understanding of the possibilities for developing learning materials.

Activity 4.7 Create learning materials

Identify an aspect of your own subject that learners find a challenge. Divide your learners into small groups and ask them to develop learning materials to help people understand the aspect. You are free to use any application or technology that you feel appropriate (e.g. eXe and Xerte).

Repositories of learning materials

In Chapter 3, repositories of learning materials were discussed with the focus on identifying content that you could use with your learners. Many repositories assume that their users are teachers seeking materials for their classes. However, some are also intended for learners to use either independently or with the encouragement of their teachers. The Open University has created a large online resource of learning materials called OpenLearn which is available at http://openlearn.open.ac.uk/.

OpenLearn contains learning materials developed for Open University students and covers a vast range of subjects and topics. It is free to all users and has discussion groups so that you can either meet other learners online or choose to learn independently. In addition to materials, it has a range of learning tools including ones to help you with re-using, re-mixing and creating content (e.g. Labspace).

Activity 4.8 OpenLearn

Explore OpenLearn with the goal of identifying content that you could adapt to meet the needs of teaching your subject. Consider how you could use the resource directly with learners, perhaps by asking them to revise some of the content.

E-books

There is considerable interest and development of electronic books. Apple has launched its iPad with the significant aim of providing a reader for all online content, including e-books. In competition with the iPad is Kindle, provided by Amazon. While this is not a new development it does seem to be gathering momentum. The JISC books project has provided further education colleges with access to 3,000 e-books for five years from April 2010. Google gives access to many millions of books, in some cases a full text version of the book.

PRACTICAL EXAMPLE – FURTHER EDUCATION E-BOOKS

The Learning and Skills Council and JISC have funded the availability of 3,000 e-books for every further education college in Great Britain for five years from April 2010 (see http://fe.jiscebooksproject.org/ or www.jisc-collections.ac.uk). The books are available at all times and can be viewed by many readers at the same time. They have been selected to meet the needs of colleges and cover vocational and academic subjects.

Webquests (C2.1 Technology)

The webquest is a learning activity developed by San Diego State University (Dodge, 2010) in 1995. It has been widely used across education with all ages of learners. It is unlike many other online activities in which learners are asked to research a topic with the aim of finding information. In a webquest, the learners are given the websites that hold the information and are asked to employ the information to achieve an objective. In this way, learners are asked to do more than simply locate information. They also have to use it.

Webquests are often used as a group activity and lots of examples have been made available on the Internet. They can be designed to focus on a specific subject or theme, making them very versatile for teaching a specialist area.

Activity 4.9 Webquest

Undertake a search of the World Wide Web (e.g. http://questgarden.com/) for examples of webquests that you could employ to teach your subject. Record their locations in your favourites and consider them carefully in order to identify one that you feel has the most promise. Use the chosen webquest with your learners and evaluate how successful it was.

Webquests can take a variety of forms. You can assign roles to each member of the group that relate to the objectives they are trying to achieve. There are relatively few limits on the tasks that you can ask learners to perform. Some examples are:

1.   Develop a business plan.
2.   Advise the government on climate change policy.
3.   What is the best approach to keeping fit?

Summary

The main points of this chapter are that:

- The post-compulsory sector includes many different contexts with associated variations in the availability of equipment and infrastructure. This has lead to different approaches being important in different parts of the sector (e.g. portability is a key factor in community-based courses).

- Each subject has its own characteristics so you need to judge what technology and approaches will be most useful for teaching it.

- E-learning, technology and your own teaching are continuously developing so it is vital to maintain your own expertise and subject understanding. Technology can assist this process by:

  - Helping you locate information through search engines
  - Finding relevant e-journals and e-newsletters
  - Participating in specialist discussion groups
  - Using online resources.

- Records of your CPD need to be kept in order to satisfy your professional responsibilities. E-portfolios can meet this need (e.g. Reflect system from the Institute for Learning).

- There are many e-learning tools and techniques that may be appropriate to your teaching objective. You need to be aware of the possibilities (e.g. blogs encourage reflection).

- The Kolb (1984) experiential learning cycle can be used to analyse tools and techniques in order to identify how you could employ them.

- It is important to evaluate, reflect and review your own use of technology to identify how you can improve its employment.

- Presenting information is a fundamental aspect of teaching. Technology can assist this task through the use of interactive whiteboards, video projectors and visualisers.

- Using video to record a face-to-face teaching session is being considered and undertaken in many areas of education and training. However, there are two main issues to resolve before recording – copyright and performing rights. It is important to take legal advice before going forward.

- Technology enables learners to be actively involved in their own learning with approaches such as developing a group report by using a wiki to jointly add and edit content.

- Technology can add fun for learners through the use of applications such as Wordle.

- Digital storytelling is a powerful and exciting method to encourage and develop creativity.

- Creating learning materials is a motivating, engaging and satisfying activity for learners. Technology provides a rich range of tools and applications to enhance the approach and allows learners to undertake work that previously was impossible or impracticable.

- Some online repositories of learning materials are open to learners to use either independently or with the encouragement of their teachers (e.g. OpenLearn – http://openlearn.open.ac.uk/).

- Webquests involve learners in the analysis and application of information they find on designated websites. They have often been used as a group activity and many examples are available on the Internet.

5

Planning for Learning

Teaching standards (LLUK, 2007)

The standard statements DS1 to DS3 with the associated technology elements D1.1 to D3.2 Technology are covered in this chapter. There is a focus on employing technology to aid and assist the planning of learning, including engaging learners in the process. There are links to other parts of the standard such as those relating to accessibility and improving learning (Chapter 3).

Introduction

Technology can help you plan and prepare for teaching and learning. It can assist in:

- Analysing needs
- Assuring equality
- Aiding the delivery of learning
- Improving the learning experience
- Allowing the learners to participate in the planning process
- Enhancing individualised learning
- Evaluating the learning process
- Helping assess your own teaching
- Adapting plans.

The key often lies in integrating technology with traditional face-to-face methods and combining formal and informal learning. Courses need to offer learners a supportive structure to give them security combined with the flexibility to manage their learning and lives. The design of the programme should encourage participation and help learners to be creative. These are not easy objectives to achieve. However, one important step is to listen to the voices of your learners. They are the most important aspect of the course and are central to its success or failure. In most cases they have considerable experience of learning and experience of different course designs. The government seeks learners' views through the National Learners' Panel and the 14 to 19 Learners' Panel. They bring together people from a wide range of courses and types of learning. Your own employer may well have their own arrangements to gain the views of learners.

Researching learners' views (D2.1 Technology; D2.2 Technology)

While it is important in the planning of education and training programmes to involve your learners in decisions, you also need to consider their experience and background before deciding on the best way to engage them. You will have different expectations if the students are coming towards the end of their course than if they are at the beginning. Technology provides a range of ways to help you consult them, including:

- Survey questionnaires
- Interviews
- Interactive consultation (e.g. voting systems)
- Management data
- E-learning literature review.

Surveying learners

Survey questionnaires have several advantages. They can be used to reach a relatively large group of people who respond in writing and so a permanent record of their views is created. However, they do have weaknesses such as you will not be able to ask follow-up or supplementary questions. They are only as good as the questions asked, so a poorly constructed question is likely to get a poor set of responses.

There are broadly two types of questions – closed and open. A closed question asks the learner to answer yes or no or to select from a series of choices indicating the strength of their response such as:

Group work is the most valuable learning experience

1. Strongly disagree
2. Disagree
3. Neither agree nor disagree
4. Agree
5. Strongly agree.

An open question requires the learners to respond with an explanation of their view such as:

How valuable are group learning activities?

Answers to closed questions can provide information in reasonable depth about the issue but only in respect of the question, which may be quite narrow. Answers to open questions offer more insight into the broader issues but they are often only answered with short statements. While closed questions can be quickly analysed, open questions can prove difficult since the respondents can write almost anything.

The normal way of constructing a questionnaire is to use both open and closed questions in order to balance their different strengths and weaknesses. In both open and closed questions, the construction of the question is critical. It is good practice to trial the survey with a small group to check that the design is effective.

PRACTICAL EXAMPLE – ONLINE SURVEYS

Two ways of creating and carrying out online surveys are:

1. Surveymonkey – this is an online resource for conducting surveys. It is free if you only use the basic service and is available at http://www.surveymonkey.com/.
2. Google Forms – this is part of Google Docs and provides a way of creating and undertaking surveys for free.

Activity 5.1 Designing questions

Create a short questionnaire with open and closed questions in order to gain the opinions of your students about which learning methods they find most effective.

What changes would you make if the learners were at the start of your course?

What changes would you make if the learners were at the end of your course?

Interviewing learners

Interviews offer a way of obtaining a rich stream of information from a group of people. However, they do have limitations, such as requiring a lot of time to perform so that often you need to restrict the number of people you interview. This tends to mean that you have to select a sample of learners to interview whereas a survey might cover them all. It is, of course, perfectly possible to combine the approaches, using the survey to gain a complete overview while employing the interview to probe the issues in more depth.

Interviews take different forms and are known as:

1. Structured: in this case all the questions are predetermined and everyone is asked the same ones. This gives a consistency to the approach and makes

analysis straightforward since everyone was asked the same questions. The predetermined questions might be decided on the results of a survey if the interview and survey approaches were being combined.

2. Semi-structured: here everyone is asked the same framework of questions but the interviewer is free to ask supplementary questions if an answer is worth probing. This combines the advantage of ease of analysis with the ability to explore selected issues in depth.

3. Open: in this case there are no set questions but each interview is unique. This allows each learner's views and experience to be explored in depth but it makes comparisons between interviews more difficult, since each takes a different form.

One challenge common to all forms of interview is that it can be difficult to ask questions, listen to answers and record the learner's responses. Often, the interview will be held up by taking notes so that a natural flow is never achieved. Technology can assist by recording the interview using an audio digital recorder or video camera. These will capture a complete record of the interview ensuring that nothing is lost. However, you should always get the agreement of the interviewee beforehand and remember that people often are influenced by being recorded.

A method that has been used to investigate e-learning approaches is the Interview Plus (Mayes, 2006). This aims to combine an interview with some other actions such as keeping a learning journal, observation or asking learners to demonstrate activities. This adds value to the interview and helps you gain a better insight into the learner's views. Observation is a valuable tool whereby you can directly witness the learner's behaviour.

For example, if you sit with learners while they undertake an activity such as participating in an online discussion, searching the Internet or making a blog entry, you can ask them questions to find out their reasons for their actions. This will help you gain an insight into their understanding and enable you to decide how best to support them. A video camera could also be employed to capture their actions. However, it is quite difficult to position a video camera to show all the small movements that are key to using a computer. It would probably be better employed showing the interaction between learners in a computer room.

Learners focus groups

A variation on a one-to-one interview is the focus group. This can be seen as a group interview where a party of learners are asked for their views, ideas and perceptions about a topic. They can be asked to experience a new teaching or learning development (e.g. course website), which is then discussed with them or they can be questioned about their experience during the course. A semi-structured approach to the questions is often followed with a set of defined questions but with the freedom to ask supplementary ones. It often requires more than one person to manage a focus group (e.g. one person asking questions with at least one notetaker). Technology can assist a focus group by using voting systems, audio and video recorders to capture reactions.

Focus groups allow the opinions of a group of learners to be explored within a relatively short time period. While this is a significant strength of the approach, the method may limit the contribution of the quieter learners and it does not allow much individual probing to take place.

Activity 5.2 Interviews versus focus groups

In your own context, when would you employ individual interviews rather than using a focus group and why?

Consulting learners

Online discussion groups can often be an effective approach to consulting with a group of learners since it allows them time to think about the issues before respond-ing to the questions posed. In addition, they can contribute to other participants' answers thus allowing a discussion to take place in which the issues are debated and analysed. As with any other online forum, it is important to moderate the discussion to encourage participation and to ensure that netiquette is followed. As the discussion is automatically recorded, you have a complete record of the consultation.

Learners management data

During the course, the learners' use of technology, such as the provider VLE, dis-cussion groups and other activities, will be logged by the system. You can identify those learners who regularly read discussion forum postings but rarely contribute. You can analyse which activities gained the most contributions and those which got the least. You have a lot of useful data to help you consider your course and to identify what needs to be improved and what were the most effective areas. It does take time to analyse this type of data and care needs to be taken to avoid jumping to conclusions.

E-learning literature review

Education and training are subjects that are heavily researched so it is important to consider the evidence from research studies that have been published. E-learning in particular, probably because of its youth, is being researched continuously. A great deal of this is published online in e-journals and websites or it can be available to download. It is always useful to look for research evidence using appropriate search engines or by visiting sector organisations (e.g. Learning and Skills Improvement Ser-vice (LSIS), JISC, LLUK, Institute for Learning and NIACE). These often support and undertake research studies in post-compulsory education. Sending an enquiry to one of the member e-mail groups that cover the sector (e.g. Association for Learning Technology (ALT)) is often effective as members tend to be supportive.

Learning design (D1.1 Technology; D1.2 Technology)

Mason and Rennie (2010) provide a clear view of learning design, suggesting that it is concerned with 'designing activities that help students learn through interaction with sources, people and ideas'. It therefore includes discussion with peers, collaboration and co-operation, researching information, creating materials and many of the other activities covered by this book. At a more basic level, course design should provide learners with:

- A structure or scaffold to assist their learning
- Opportunities to learn through active engagement (i.e. by doing)
- Clear objectives that relate to the activities, methods and assessment included in the course.

Instruction has been summarised as 'show, tell and do'. This means that learners need the opportunity to be shown relevant examples of what they are studying, have issues told or explained to them and then are able to practise or carry out tasks. A fourth stage, that of checking, has often been added to this process. This can take a variety of forms, including review, assess or reflect. Technology can support and enhance the whole process and for the most effective outcomes, you need to consider systematically what you are trying to achieve. Cercone (2008) offers a range of characteristics that will aid the design of effective online courses for adults. They include:

- Taking a learner-centred approach
- Supporting learners to become self-reliant
- Building on learners' prior knowledge and skills
- Using learning related to learners' needs
- Encouraging collaboration and co-operation
- Providing an appropriate challenge for learners
- Assisting learners to reflect on their learning experiences.

Although these are focused on adult learners in an online environment, they are also clearly applicable to other groups and classroom settings. Table 5.1 shows a breakdown of design features and e-learning methods. There are a large number of possible approaches and many serve a range of purposes. Because it is always important to employ your chosen methods to their full potential, it is probably sensible to use a limited number so as to develop your own expertise in their use. Methods can serve a range of uses. A portfolio can be the focus for the assessment of the course (i.e. both formative and summative) while also encouraging self-reliance, providing opportunities for reflection, offering a means to develop peer co-operation (e.g. feedback on each other's evidence) and also demonstrating long-term benefits of learning to the learner (e.g. help to create a CV). In order to realise this potential, you need to understand each functional area of the portfolio and to integrate it into the course.

TABLE 5.1 Design features and e-learning

FEATURES	METHODS AND APPROACHES	COMMENTS
Show	1. Multimedia 2. Video 3. Interactive whiteboard 4. Microsoft PhotoStory 5. Visualisers	There is a wide range of technological aids to help you show or demonstrate to a class or group of learners. It is important that you can use them confidently or you may damage your credibility with the learners.
Tell	1. Presentation application 2. Podcasts 3. Handouts 4. Recording lecture 5. Virtual classrooms 6. Interactive whiteboards 7. VLEs 8. Learning materials	There are many different approaches that can support presenting information to learners. It is important to consider the overall approach of the course. A mainly face-to-face programme would probably centre on classroom-based methods such as interactive whiteboards. A programme aimed at learners studying in geographically dispersed locations may well employ virtual classrooms and podcasts.
Do/Active learning	1. Online projects 2. Digital cameras to record experiences 3. Creating learning materials 4. Webquests 5. Discussion groups	Using technology can often provide a motivating experience to a learner (e.g. recording a field trip with a video camera). Online communication tools can offer groups of learners the means to work together on a project.
Learner-centred	1. Creating learning materials 2. Online materials 3. Online discussion groups 4. Mobile learning	E-learning approaches offer learners opportunities to engage in activities such as using authoring tools to create materials. This both motivates them and gives them a focus to explore a subject and develop their understanding of it.
Self-reliance	1. Portfolio 2. Mobile learning 3. Self-testing	One of the characteristics of successful participants in online learning is self-reliance. It is also a feature that many employers value in employees.

TABLE 5.1 (continued)

FEATURES	METHODS AND APPROACHES	COMMENTS
Collaboration and co-operation	1. Discussion forums 2. Webquests 3. Voting systems 4. Wikis	It is not enough to simply provide the means for collaboration and co-operation. They must be supported by giving the learners strong reasons to participate.
Reflection	1. Learning diaries/blogs 2. Portfolios	Reflection is a difficult skill for learners to master so alongside the e-learning approach must be the support to enable them to develop.
Assessment	1. Portfolio 2. Voting systems 3. Online questionnaire 4. Multiple choice questions	Providing the means for the learners to test themselves will encourage them to become more responsible for their own development. E-assessment approaches can provide more flexibility so that learners can choose to be tested when they are ready, rather than at a set time.

Learning styles

People prefer to learn in different ways. Some like to learn through active approaches that involve taking part in activities while others prefer to listen to teachers or read material. There are several models of learning styles that propose different types of preferences. E-learning has the potential to offer a range of alternative methods of learning so that learners can choose the way that they prefer.

For example, a course could offer to deliver information through:

1. Face-to-face lecture
2. Podcast
3. Internet-based project
4. VLE stored handouts.

By offering alternatives you will be meeting the needs of the different learning styles and also providing more flexibility and choice to the learners.

Integration of formal, informal and mobile learning (D2.1 Technology; D2.2 Technology)

A key aspect in the planning and design of learning programmes is how to integrate formal, informal and mobile learning to maximise their different strengths. It is always tempting to make almost everything formal because you are often working with a defined curriculum, qualification syllabus or other external constraints. These can be helpful in that they are accompanied by ideas, approaches and methods from awarding bodies, sector skills councils or others based on good practice. Yet even in these cases you will have considerable freedom of how to plan your course.

There are considerable advantages in giving learners responsibility and freedom to choose their own approaches to reaching the course objectives. They will be more likely to be motivated and will have the opportunity to develop independent learning skills. This freedom must be judged carefully in terms of the learners and activity being undertaken. It needs to take them forward without too many risks of failure. The formal learning can provide the structure and scaffolding for the learners to climb so that their own choices are the natural next ones.

Mobile learning has the potential to allow the learners more freedom as to where, when and how they learn. It is therefore a natural part of the formal, informal and mobile integration process. Within the formal structure, there is a need to provide opportunities for the learners to select a mobile method (e.g. providing written and audio learning materials).

The key is to consider all the options when planning so that you offer opportunities in a safe and supportive environment that allows the learners to grow. This implies that you are doing things to the learners but it is far more effective to negotiate their personal objectives and degree of freedom. Technology can play an important role in this process in a variety of ways such as:

- Providing them with a draft of the plan to comment or to amend with track changes
- Establishing an online discussion group for everyone to debate the plans
- Asking learners to create personal learning plans for the course, identifying their goals in order for you to agree them. Electronic plans allow you to alter them during the course if the situation changes (e.g. electronic individual learning plans e-ILP).

Activity 5.3 Mind mapping

Mind mapping can be a useful way of considering the planning of a course. It allows you to integrate formal, informal and mobile learning. Using one of the mind mapping applications listed in the Tools appendix (e.g. FreeMind), develop an overall plan for the course.

Show the mind map plan to your learners and ask them individually or in small groups to provide you with feedback and consider their personal learning objectives in undertaking the course.

Evaluation (D3.1 Technology; D3.2 Technology)

In the context of planning, you can consider either evaluating your use of technology to help the processes or using technology to assist the evaluation of your planning. Technology provides a record of its use so that if you are employing it to help you plan you can later review the process to evaluate it. It also offers the potential for a continuous process of evaluation rather than one that takes place at the end of the course. Continuous evaluation allows you to make improvements during the course. It is immediate and can address issues without having to wait for the next course.

Evaluation approaches

There are three approaches to evaluation that you may wish to consider:

- Peer review
- Learner review
- Self-review.

Peer review is widely used in many different parts of education and training. It is often included in quality assurance systems with colleagues bringing expertise in planning, delivery and teaching of the subject or similar to bear on evaluating and reviewing. McNaught (2001) describes the use of peer reviews as part of evaluating and improving online course development, providing peers with a checklist of criteria to focus their review.

Learner review is an important element in any learning and is probably most effective if undertaken throughout the course. Planning is thus a continuous process with improvement integrated into it. Learner review can be undertaken in a similar way to peer review, employing a checklist to provide a framework for the learners to consider. This is often helpful in focusing the attention of the reviewers but there is the risk that aspects not included in the criteria will be ignored. Learners are often effective when identifying issues not obvious to the teaching staff, so care must be taken to encourage learners to feedback on everything and not simply the criteria.

Self-review, i.e. self-assessment, is emphasised as part of the CPD now required of all teachers. You may want to employ a learning journal (e.g. blog) to reflect on your planning as well as your other experiences. This should obviously consider the outcomes of the peer and learner reviews. Reflection is another continuous process, so that evaluation of planning is again ongoing and not a once-a-course activity.

Activity 5.4 Review criteria

Consider the criteria for the review of your planning process by your peers and learners. Develop a short list of the key factors that you would like each group to use. In particular, how can technology assist the review?

Assisting all learners to participate (D2.1 Technology; D2.2 Technology)

Technology provides the means to help all learners participate and gain access to learning. It can remove or lower barriers that in previous generations have prevented or limited participation. However, these potential benefits are not achieved unless the learning programmes are carefully planned so as to identify and employ appropriate methods and technologies in the design of the education and training programmes. The learning activities should be improved for all learners.

How e-learning relates to learning objectives

Bloom (1956) suggested three types of learning objective. These were:

- Cognitive
- Psychomotor
- Affective.

In simpler terms, these are knowledge, skills and attitudes. All three types can be supported by technology in different ways and to different degrees of effectiveness.

Knowledge has two main components – information and understanding. Technology has enormous power to provide access to information covering almost every subject. The World Wide Web can be considered to be one immense library of information with easy access through a search engine. However, there are limitations. The learners need good search skills to locate the information they are seeking, combined with information literacy so that they evaluate the quality and appropriateness of the information.

Access to information is not sufficient. For the learners to gain understanding, they need to use the information to achieve a purpose, thereby gaining experience and understanding. Learners may need to understand the individual tax system in the country. It is relatively straightforward to locate information about tax rates, allowances, exceptions and other conditions but this does not guarantee the learners' understanding of the system. However, if locating the information is combined with an activity such as creating a spreadsheet to calculate the tax liability of several different people then understanding should grow through learning by doing.

Understanding is also developed through discussion of the issues to consider different aspects. An online forum discussing the tax system may well probe the justice and fairness of the system and take the learners' understanding beyond the application of the system to calculate individuals' tax payments. A webquest could be created to explore alternative approaches to personal taxes so that understanding is again enhanced. The starting learning objective is the deciding factor in which learning activities, and thus e-learning approaches, are needed. For example:

1. Information
At the end of the activity, learners should be able to quote the personal tax allowance and basic rate of tax.
Activity: Search the Internet for information.

2. Basic understanding
At the end of the activity, learners should be able to calculate the tax paid by a person earning the average wage in Great Britain.
Activities: Search the Internet for information.
   Use a spreadsheet to calculate tax payment.

3. Enhance understanding
At the end of the activity, learners should be able to discuss the impact of raising the threshold of personal allowances compared with reducing the basic rate of tax.
Activities: Search the Internet for information.
   Participate in a webquest to role play a treasury committee charged with improving the income of low-paid families by either raising the personal allowance or decreasing the basic rate of tax.

Activity 5.5 Information

Consider your subject and design a learning activity linked to an appropriate objective that involves the learners locating relevant information.

Activity 5.6 Understanding

Consider the learning objective you developed in the previous activity and extend it so that the learners not only locate the relevant information but also use it in a way that promotes understanding.

Learning needs

The planning and design of your learning activities is directly related to the learning objective you are aiming to achieve. They also need to consider the needs of your learners. If the webquest we decided was appropriate to develop understanding took place face-to-face, that may well be appropriate in many situations. However, if some of the group were carers and unable to travel then they would be excluded from the activity. You need to consider your learners' needs as you design your course. In this case, switching the activity to an online forum would allow everyone to participate. However, a face-to-face webquest might take an afternoon to complete while an asynchronous discussion forum webquest would probably be spread over a few weeks. It is always important to realise that all changes have consequences that you need to consider.

Developing learners' skills

The development of skills involves learners in being able to carry out physical tasks, which at first glance does not appear to require technology. However, simulations can be very effective in helping learners develop the required skills and, at an early stage in the process, ensure their safety. In any environment learners are at risk due to their lack of experience and so a simulation can be used to help provide them with enough experience to reduce the risk. Many basic simulations ask learners to explore an environment in order to identify the potential health and safety hazards as in the theory aspect of a driving test. Other uses of simulations are:

■ ICT skills development (e.g. mouse simulation)
■ Business models
■ Manufacturing process management
■ Interviewing and communication skills
■ Science simulations.

Technology can be used to capture learners' practice thus allowing more effective feedback to be given using video or still images that show them how to improve. Observation is a normal teaching process but it can be difficult at times to provide clear feedback of a physical process. Video offers a powerful means of showing the learners what they are doing and how to improve. Without video, the teacher will probably need to demonstrate the correct process, which the learners need to watch and interpret. While it is not always possible to provide an exact demonstration every time, video allows you to capture a perfect one.

Activity 5.7 Skills

Consider your subject and design a learning activity linked to an appropriate objective that involves the learners in developing a skill that employs technology to aid the process.

Developing learners' attitudes

The learners' attitudes are often a key factor in employability. Employers often place considerable value of the learners' ability to:

■ Work in a team (e.g. interpersonal skills)
■ Communicate effectively through listening, speaking and writing
■ Be analytical, considering priorities to identify what they should do
■ Be self-starters (e.g. organise, adapt and motivate themselves)
■ Be dependable and reliable

- Be self-confident
- Be willing to learn.

Almost all these factors relate to the personal attitudes of the employee. Vocational courses or those that relate to employment need to consider how to develop learners' attitudes. This can often be achieved through learning activities such as group work that will help develop team working and relationship-related attitudes. E-learning can provide a focus for team working (e.g. webquests), help motivate learners, develop self-confidence and offer opportunities to improve their communication (e.g. discussion forums, virtual classrooms etc.). Attitudes are often developed through interaction with other learners and technology can be effective in creating a suitable environment. In face-to-face situations, the more extrovert participants can often dominate the communication and activity, whereas online communications are more open so that individuals cannot so easily take over the situation.

Activity 5.8 Attitudes

Consider your subject and design a learning activity linked to an appropriate objective that involves the learners developing their attitudes and that employs technology to aid the process.

Integration of resources

It requires careful planning to gain the most effective use of technology in learning activities. In particular, you need to consider how to integrate your resources and tools in order to achieve your objectives. Examples are:

1. Combine the use of mind mapping applications with an online information gathering project to explore fully the subjects and key words that must be used when searching the World Wide Web for appropriate content.
2. Use voting technology to encourage participation in a discussion of a topic prior to a presentation that uses an interactive whiteboard.
3. Divide learners into small groups to research a subject in order to create a podcast.

E-learning strategies

You will not be working in isolation when seeking to employ e-learning. The majority of educational and training providers in the post-compulsory education sector have created e-learning or ILT strategies. It is important to check what the overall strategy is for your organisation. It may indicate priorities and approaches that you will need to adopt and thus save you time and effort.

Comparing synchronous and asynchronous communication

Communication technologies are central to e-learning and all of them have benefits and limitations. There are many types of communication technology and one broad way of dividing them is into synchronous and asynchronous. Those like a telephone conversation with participants present at the same time is synchronous and those where participants can read and send messages at any time such as e-mail are asynchronous. Table 5.2 compares the two approaches.

Assumptions about learners

While it is often the case that we assume learners are skilled users of all technology, the digital divide is still evident in society. JISC (2007), reporting on research to consider the opinion of e-learning among learners in further and higher education, stated that some learners needed assistance with the technologies used in their institutions.

TABLE 5.2 Comparing synchronous and asynchronous communication technologies

COMMUNICATION CHARACTERISTIC	SYNCHRONOUS	ASYNCHRONOUS
One-to-one	Many methods had their origin in this way and are effective communications methods.	Methods are designed for one-to-one communication.
One-to-many	Some synchronous methods allow you to broadcast messages (e.g. text messaging).	Asynchronous approaches are often employed to send messages to lots of people.
Many-to-many	Some methods such as video and audio conferencing can be used in this way but others are clearly not suitable (e.g. text messaging). However, even the appropriate approaches have limitations on the size of the group.	Discussion forums do provide a means for groups to communicate. However, it can become confusing if the group is large.
Immediate	These methods are designed to provide immediate and direct communication.	There is an unpredictable delay in waiting for messages to be read and responded to.
Decision making	This can be fast since everyone is present and able to contribute.	Can take a long time since participants have the freedom to participate when it is convenient for them.
Convenience	These methods do require everyone to agree on the time of communication and thus it will have an impact on individuals.	Methods enable users to communicate when it is most appropriate for them and it allows them to manage their time.
Reflection	Synchronous methods are immediate so there is little time to reflect on your contributions.	These methods allow users time to consider their contributions and weigh the messages from other participants.

Equally, some learners expected technology to be used in their courses. This shows there are still considerable differences in the skills, attitudes towards and experience of people with respect to technology. If planning to use e-learning with your learners, you need to consider their reaction to its application and also its limited use.

It is not always easy to know what a learner's reaction will be to the use of technology. The stereotype is to assume that all younger learners will be positive towards technology, expecting or not being surprised by its use. That, however, does not mean they have experience of using it for learning in the way that you intend to employ it. Older learners may be assumed to have poor technological skills, but many older people welcome the opportunity to learn through and about technology and so may be well motivated towards e-learning.

E-learning is also not simply about technology. It also requires learners to have the appropriate learning skills, such as reflection, writing and communication. You will need to consider whether they will already have the necessary skills and how you are going to support their development.

In planning to use e-learning you need to consider:

- The expectations and attitudes of your learners to the use of technology in their course
- The technical skills of your learners
- The e-learning skills of your learners
- How you will support the development of the required skills.

Activity 5.9 Learners' attitudes

Consider how two different groups of learners, first, a group of 18-year-olds studying for Advanced Level GCSEs, and second, a group of over-50-year-olds seeking to improve their literacy, would react to:

1. Using a blog to develop a learning diary
2. Participating in an asynchronous discussion forum
3. Producing a report using Microsoft PowerPoint.

How would you introduce the technology to achieve the best results in both cases?

Disabled learners and learners with learning difficulties

Technology can be used to assist disabled learners and those with learning difficulties overcome some of the barriers they face, but it can also be another barrier, depending on how it is employed. The SENDA 2001 (Office of Public Sector Information, n.d.) extended the DDA into education. It is an offence for disabled learners to be treated in a less favourable way than other learners, and providers must make 'reasonable adjustments' to ensure disabled learners are not disadvantaged. It is therefore important to consider the impact of technology on your learners when you are planning the course. An obvious way of doing this is to consult with the learners about their needs.

This is a specialist area in which you will need to seek advice and guidance from your provider and other agencies. The Techdis website provides support for teachers using e-learning, to ensure that the benefits of technology are realised for disabled learners. It includes guidelines for the creation of e-learning content and self-assessment accessibility tools plus links to many other sources such as advice on assistive technologies. The Techdis Accessibility Essentials Series (Techdis, 2007) offers advice and guidance that is key reading for anyone seeking to gain the benefits of technology for disabled learners.

Activity 5.10 Actions

There are many different ways of using technology to assist disabled learners and people with learning difficulties. Consider your own experience of learners and visit the Techdis Accessibility Series to identify some approaches that you could employ.

PRACTICAL EXAMPLE – BROWSEALOUD

BrowseAloud (www.browsealoud.com) is a tool to read aloud website contents including PDFs and word documents. It is aimed at helping learners with limited literacy skills, a visual impairment or who are learning English as a second language.

PRACTICAL EXAMPLE – MICROSOFT WINDOWS

Microsoft Windows provides a range of accessibility options to customise the system. These include:

1. An onscreen magnifier
2. Adjusting the display to make it easier to read
3. Help with using a keyboard and mouse
4. Screen reader.

Summary

The main points of this chapter are:

- Planning learning is concerned with integrating technology with traditional face-to-face methods and combining formal and informal learning.

- Courses need to offer learners a supportive structure to provide security, flexibility, and to encourage participation and creativity.

- It is important to engage your learners in the planning and design and this involves you understanding their experience and background.

- Technology provides a range of ways of consulting learners such as survey questionnaires, interviews, management data and interactive consultation (e.g. voting systems).

- Questionnaires can be used to reach a relatively large group of people but it is not possible to ask follow-up or supplementary questions.

- Interviews can obtain a rich stream of information from learners but do require a lot of time and can only cover a sample of learners.

- Mason and Rennie (2010) suggest that design is concerned with 'designing activities that help students learn through interaction with sources, people and ideas'. The design of a course needs to include a structure or scaffold to assist learning, opportunities for active engagement and clear objectives.

- People prefer to learn in different ways (e.g. active, listening and reading material). E-learning can offer a range of alternative ways of learning to meet learners' preferences.

- A key aspect of planning and design of learning programmes is how to integrate formal, informal and mobile learning to maximise their different strengths.

- Formal learning can offer learners the structure and scaffolding to support them while informal learning can assist them to take responsibility for their learning. Mobile learning provides learners with increased freedom to choose where, when and how they learn.

- Technology can assist you to evaluate your planning and your use of technology.

- Technology can continuously record its use providing you with useful planning information.

- There are three approaches to evaluation that you may use. They are peer review, learner review and self-review.

- Technology can assist all learners to participate and access learning. In order to gain these benefits requires carefully planning to identify and employ appropriate methods and technologies in the design of programmes.

- Bloom (1956) suggested three types of learning objective. These are cognitive, psychomotor and affective or, in simpler terms, knowledge, skills and attitudes.

- Technology can offer access to information covering almost every subject. Communication technologies offer the means to discuss and analyse information to improve understanding.

- Simulations can be very effective in helping learners to develop skills safely.

- Attitudes can often be developed through collaborative group working.

- Communication technologies can be classified as synchronous and asynchronous. Each has its strengths and weaknesses.

- It is dangerous to make assumptions about the technical skills of learners. They will vary considerably from expert to novice depending on the technology being considered.
- The SENDA 2001 (Office of Public Sector Information, n.d.) extended the DDA into education. These make it an offence for disabled learners to be treated in a less favourable way than other learners and providers must make 'reasonable adjustments' to ensure disabled learners are not disadvantaged.

6

Assessment for Learning

Teaching standards (LLUK, 2007)

The standard statements ES1 to ES5 with the associated technology elements E1.1 to E5.1 Technology are covered in this chapter. These are focused on the use of technology to assess learning, covering both formative and summative assessment. Chapter 2 and 3 also provide relevant content.

Introduction

There has been a significant growth in e-assessment, that is, employing technology to assess learners' progress and achievement. Technology has been used to enhance both formative and summative assessment. Formative is essentially that of assessing learners' progress, enabling the teacher, themselves or their peers to provide feedback so as to improve their performance. Summative is concerned with the final assessment and is often linked to the achievement of a qualification. Many awarding bodies offer summative e-assessment for some of their qualifications. Probably one of the widest used is the Driving Theory Test, which employs a multiple-choice questioning approach. The interest in using e-assessment amongst awarding bodies was identified several years ago (Thomson, 2005).

There are many e-assessment approaches, including:

1. Multiple-choice questions – technology can be used to automate the process and randomise the selection of questions. Technology-supported multiple choice is widely used and in a variety of ways. For example:

    a. Only one choice is displayed at a time so learners are required to make their selection without the benefit of seeing all the optional answers.

    b. Questions can be selected from a bank on a random basis.

These types of tests can be marked by the computer, providing an almost instant result for the learner and removing the marking burden from the teacher. However, multiple-choice questions are mainly suitable for assessing knowledge.

2. E-portfolios have been widely used as a means of compiling a portfolio of evidence electronically to demonstrate a learner's competence. However, they can be used more widely as a lifelong learning repository of achievements, to enhance learning through formative feedback, to record and improve CPD and as a form of electronic CV.

    Importantly, e-assessment can provide on-demand tests so that learners can request their assessment when they are ready rather than at fixed times during the year. This has the potential to increasing the flexibility of the system. Interest in this area is growing rapidly with Ofqual, the regulatory authority, publishing two reports (Ofqual, 2010a; 2010b) on the subject in 2010.

E-assessment tools and approaches (E1.1 Technology; E3.1 Technology)

There are many different tools and approaches that can be used for both formative and summative assessment. This includes providing feedback, self-assessment, reflecting on performance, peer review and diagnostic tools. E-portfolios have received considerable attention and have been used extensively across the different education sectors, in relation to many different subjects and at a range of educational levels.

E-portfolios

E-portfolios are collections of digital evidence that show the learners' skills, knowledge and understanding. They have a number of advantages over paper or conventional portfolios in that they can hold video and digital images, text, audio, blog entries and any other digital item. They are often stored online so that material can be uploaded from different locations (e.g. workplace, college and home) and capacity is not limited.

E-portfolios have been divided into four types. These are:

1. Assessment
2. Developmental
3. Reflective
4. Showcasing.

Assessment portfolios, as the name suggests, are focused on collecting evidence to demonstrate that the learner has the skills, knowledge and competency to meet a particular standard. They are almost always part of a final or summative assessment and a variety of bespoke products have been developed to help learners achieve a particular qualification. The specific evidence requirements are normally tightly defined so that they clearly show the learner's ability. The evidence requirements may include:

- Witness statements from supervisors, mangers, training officers, etc., testifying to the skills and ability of the learner
- Video and still images showing skills
- Evidence of carrying out tasks satisfactorily.

In some cases, the presentation of evidence is defined in that the number, length and type of evidence are limited.

Developmental portfolios are collections of evidence that show the learner's growth, development and improvement. They are often used by professional staff seeking to show that they are enhancing their skills, knowledge and understanding. They could also be part of a trainee or apprentice programme where it is important to demonstrate that they are acquiring the skills and understanding. The evidence is often chosen to show the distance travelled and can take the form of performance assessments, witness statements and examples of tasks completed.

Reflective portfolios are intended to provide the opportunity to enhance your own reflections on your experience. It may include a blog to help you reflect and allow peers and tutors to comment on your reviews. Again, it is a collection of evidence with an obvious emphasis on reflection. It may include learning agreements, plans, reviews, blog entries and formative feedback. One document is the reflective commentary, in which a learner is asked to reflect on an overall learning experience. Reflection involves comparing and contrasting experiences with each other. Critical analysis of what went well and what were the weaknesses are key, along with judging how to improve the learner's behaviour.

Showcasing portfolios were probably the original portfolio, in that they are intended to be examples of the individual's best work. Artists, for example, would select items of their work to impress prospective employers, clients and others. In a wide sense, a showcase e-portfolio serves the same purpose of a collection of a person's work aimed to providing a reference. The main difference is that there is no limit to the size of a showcase e-portfolio. From a large collection, a smaller collection can be produced for a specific purpose (e.g. a CV created for a particular job). A showcase e-portfolio can thus produce many different collections.

In certain situations you will want aspects of more than one type of portfolio and this is perfectly possible with systems such as Pebblepad (http://www.pebblepad.co.uk/) and Mahara (http://mahara.org/), which have been designed to provide for all four types. Users are free to select the aspects of the system that are most appropriate to their needs.

Activity 6.1 Exploring e-portfolios

There is a wide range of e-portfolio systems available and it is important to understand what they can offer you as a teacher, tutor or trainer. Mahara (http://mahara.org/) is an open source system while PebblePad (http://www.pebblepad.co.uk/) is a commercial product. Explore each system through the demonstrations and other resources on their respective websites. Figure 6.1 shows the Mahara website.

Alternatively, try the e-portfolio used in your college or provider. It is important to consider:

1. Customising the interface to meet personal preferences
2. The speed of operation
3. Uploading and creating content
4. Sharing content with other users
5. Providing feedback on content
6. Creating collections of evidence for assessment or other purposes.

Compare two or more systems. They will often use different terminology to describe content and other features.

FIGURE 6.1 Mahara website

Collections of evidence

The central element in an e-portfolio is the collection of evidence. This is not simply a random pile of documents, recordings and other digital resources but a carefully selected set of evidence that aims to meet a distinct purpose. The exact purpose will depend on the type of portfolio the learner is developing.

An assessment portfolio will need a clear framework of the learning objectives, outcomes or competences that the learner is seeking to achieve. The collection will need to align with the elements of the framework that will often provide distinct guidelines for the nature of the evidence that is required. For example:

- Only items arising from activities in the last three years
- Witness statements from senior managers
- No more than two items of evidence for each learning objective claimed.

A learner will develop his or her collection through the learning programme and it will be influenced by the portfolio processes of reflection, peer assessment, feedback and review (Figure 6.2). The resulting evidence will need to be mapped against the assessment framework to select the evidence for the summative assessment. Normally, in addition to the evidence, the learner is required to provide some overview statements such as an explanation of context and how each item demonstrates his or her achievement of the assessment framework elements.

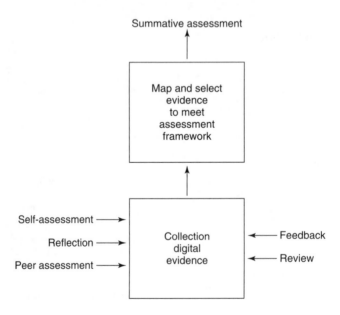

FIGURE 6.2 Summative assessment

A development portfolio often has a long-term aim with evidence seeking to show the distance travelled in acquiring and maintaining professional skills, knowledge and understanding. It is potentially a lifelong collection, so it is important that it is well-structured with items easily located. Some professional bodies now require members to present evidence to demonstrate their CPD.

A reflective portfolio is intended to help learners reflect on their experiences in order to achieve deep learning. It is not normally limited to personal reflections only, but will also provide opportunities for peers and teachers to provide comments on work done and their reflections on the learning experience. This type of portfolio is largely aimed at helping the individual learner who may limit those that have access to its contents. A reflective portfolio can obviously play a role in the other three types and many professional bodies now require members to become reflective practitioners, able to learn from their sexperience. This type of portfolio can obviously serve as evidence that a learner is a reflective practitioner.

A showcase portfolio is the original type that has been used for generations to demonstrate artists', architects' and others' abilities through presenting a range of their work. Its limitation was principally its size – there were obviously limits on how large a portfolio you could carry. E-portfolios have overcome this problem since digital resources can be stored in very large quantities. A showcase portfolio can hold hundreds or even thousands of items. However, it would be unreasonable to expect an employer or other person viewing the showcase to look at more than a few. It is therefore important that showcase portfolios have the means of creating a subset of the collection precisely focused on a specific need (e.g. applying for a particular job) so that the viewer need only consider the directly relevant items selected by the portfolio owner. The need to select items also requires that they are stored in a structured way and can be searched for particular pieces. This may mean the need to tag them with keywords so that they can be easily searched. This in turn means that learners need to understand tagging or another alternative means of structuring the evidence.

Discussion of the different types is helpful in understanding e-portfolios. However, it is important to realise that many systems combine the different types of portfolio into a single integrated system that allows you to undertake all the activities.

PRACTICAL EXAMPLE – GOOGLE APPS FOR EDUCATION

Google has made its applications available to schools, colleges and universities to allow students access to a set of tools that will enable them to create, share, present, communicate and store information. These tools could be used to create a portfolio for each learner.

Activity 6.2 Exploring Google Apps

Explore the tools available in Google Apps and consider how they could contribute to creating a portfolio. You might consider how learners would:

1. Store all types of information (e.g. documents, images, audio and video)
2. Collaborate with other learners and teachers
3. Be assessed on their portfolios
4. Present their portfolios
5. Reflect on their experiences
6. Do anything else.

Formative and summative assessment

You can divide assessment into two main types:

1. Formative
2. Summative.

Formative is intended to help the learners improve their performance by providing feedback to them on the work they have undertaken. Technology often has the potential to provide focused feedback to the learner. An e-portfolio offers a variety of opportunities to help learners by reviewing the quality of their evidence, commenting on learning diary blogs and identifying strengths and weaknesses. The feedback can come both from you and also from peers or other sources (e.g. managers). Many e-portfolio systems provide the means for learners to share their work with designated people. Figure 2.1 identified several routes for formative assessment feedback in an e-portfolio system such as:

■ Sharing
■ Collaborating
■ Dialogue (e.g. discussion).

Summative assessment is intended to be the final judgement on the learners' performance. In respect of an e-portfolio, the learner presents a collection of evidence that meets a set of defined competencies or other characteristics. These are often national standards and need to be clear, unambiguous statements of what is needed. If you are defining your own assessment characteristics then you need to be sure they are detailed and comprehensible. Figure 6.3 illustrates some of the processes that can take place in relation to an e-portfolio that contributes to formative assessment.

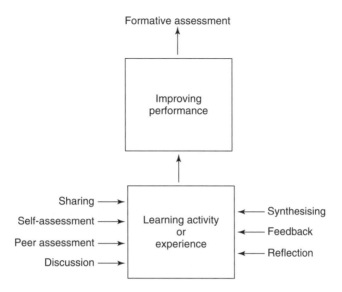

FIGURE 6.3 Formative assessment processes

Ownership of e-portfolios

One critical factor concerns the ownership of e-portfolio content. In many situations assessments are the property of the college or educational provider. In the case of an e-portfolio, this can be a problem since the learners may wish to build on it during their career or transfer it to a new educational provider. Learners have to put a substantial effort into building a portfolio and one of its key benefits is that it will have other uses apart from the assessment for the course (e.g. lifelong record of achievement). However, even if the ownership issue is resolved, there are often technological limitations. Many e-portfolios are embedded within other systems, for example, the institution's VLE. This is likely to mean that the format of the contents is incompatible with other systems.

One solution to the problem of transfer is to create and store the portfolio as a cloud resource, that is, online, so that the learners can access the material from anywhere they have access to the Internet. However, this does raise questions of security of the content since it is now outside the direct control of the educational or training provider. Google Apps offers a cloud storage system that is free for providers to use in support of their educational activities. It comes with security features built in.

Learning diaries

Many professions, such as nursing, are now seeking to develop reflective practitioners and in any occupation it is vital to develop yourself through learning from your experiences. Reflecting on experience is key to deep learning and your own development. One approach to encouraging reflection is the use of a learning diary. This functions like a conventional diary in that you record your experiences, what you have learnt and how that relates to other experiences. You try to make judgements and arrive at conclusions. It is not easy to write a reflective learning diary or journal, but one way that technology can help is through a blog in which peers, mentors and tutors can offer comments on your reflections, so helping you improve. Learning diaries or journals often form part of an e-portfolio system.

Study plan

Most educational or training institutions will provide learners with a study plan informing them of deadlines, course details and assessments. This is valuable to the learner but of course it is general and cannot take into account the learner's other priorities such as work, family and other courses they may be undertaking in parallel. There are several technological ways of producing an individual study plan, including Microsoft Outlook Calendar and Google Calendar. Both Outlook and Google Calendars allow a personalised plan to be produced, with Google offering the additional advantage of also being available online so it can be accessed from anywhere.

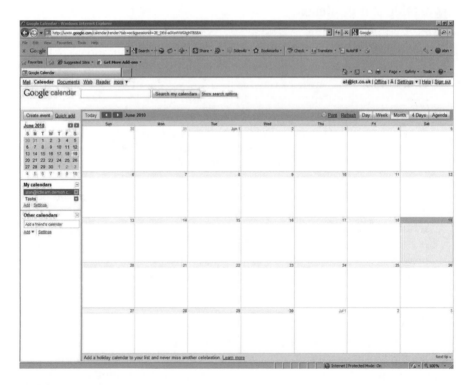

FIGURE 6.4 Google Calendar

Activity 6.3 Study plan

Gain experience of using either Microsoft Outlook, Google Calendar or another option to create a plan of your own work load, family and other commitments. Identify what you feel would be the main issues for your learners when using the same application to produce a personalised study plan.

Tests

It is important to remember when creating tests that you need a question or task that, if successfully answered or completed, means that the learner has achieved the objective. This is not straightforward and it can be quite difficult to develop this type of question or activity. Nevertheless, it is very useful to have a test since it can be used not only as the concluding assessment at the end of the course but also as an initial assessment to help develop the individual learning plan.

Tests can serve many purposes such as:

- Initial assessment
- Measure progress
- Final examination
- Self-assessment.

You need to consider what type of test is appropriate for the objective you are assessing. The main types of test used in e-assessment are:

- True or false
- Selecting between two options
- Multiple choice
- Select the right answer or answers from a list of options
- Complete the blanks in a sentence or passage
- Make links between two sets of items
- Place objects or items into the right order
- Write your answer
- Undertake a task.

A test can be employed not only as an assessment but also as a learning activity to help learners develop their knowledge, skills and attitudes. It is motivating to see their scores improve.

Voting technology

Betts and Kambouri (2007) undertook an action research project to consider the use of voting technology in assessing adult literacy and numeracy. They came to a number of interesting conclusions:

- The process encourages learners to ask questions and discuss issues between questions.

- It helps identify weaknesses and thus allows future sessions to be changed to focus on them.

- Assessment questions need to be developed meticulously to ensure they are testing what you intend.

- Most learners enjoyed the assessment process but some limitations, such as not being able to check and revise answers, were identified.

Using voting technology can be both motivating and fun for the learners and is an effective way to gain feedback quickly from a whole group. It does, however, have some limitations, such as not allowing the learners to change their answers on reviewing them.

Text walls are similar to voting technology as they allow learners to text their feedback to a website that collects and presents all the comments. It is normal practice to display the feedback so that all learners can see what their peers have said. A second stage of the process is to invite the learners to send follow-up messages responding to their peers' messages.

Peer assessment

E-learning methods and techniques are often aimed at helping the learners to become more independent and self-sufficient. It is therefore appropriate if, alongside these developments, they also take some responsibility for assessing themselves. Peer assessment is often employed in group and project work. It can take many forms but each learner may be asked to mark their peers in terms of their contribution to the exercise, discussion or activity. The assessment can provide each person with formative feedback to help improve all or part of the final marks (i.e. summative assessment). In a sense, it helps learners to see themselves as their peers see them, giving the learners some degree of ownership of the assessment process.

There are practical difficulties in providing peer assessment such as:

- How accurate is the assessment (e.g. learners may have little experience of assessing others)?

- How will the learners' interpersonal relationships with each other influence their assessment?

- Is the assessment anonymous?

Technology can be used to provide peer assessment in a variety of ways, including:

- Using comments and track changes to give feedback
- Adding comments to peers' blogs (i.e. learning journals)
- Giving direct feedback through e-mail.

To help learners provide peer assessment, they will need specific criteria on which to mark their colleagues and, just as importantly, on how to give the feedback. This will assist in overcoming their lack of assessment experience.

Diagnostic tools

There are many different diagnostic tools that enable you to assess individuals, groups or even whole organisations. There are also tools to help you create specific tests and assessments. Diagnostic tests are often concerned with assessing any specific learning weaknesses that a learner may have.

Tests cover a range of issues such as:

- Literacy and numeracy
- Dyslexia
- Learning styles.

The outcomes of the tests are often useful in helping you customise the learning experience for the individual. Many colleges and other providers employ diagnostic tests during the induction process as an initial assessment. However, the results of diagnostic tests require skilled interpretation, so it is important to check that you understand the outcome of the test.

In addition to diagnostic tests, there are many assessment systems aimed at particular subjects that can be used by an individual as a self-test. However, it is important to try them out to ensure they are assessing your subject correctly and that they can be used many times since learners often want to test themselves repeatedly. There is little value in learners testing themselves against the same questions over and over again. Systems are often based around a database of different tests that are randomly selected each time someone takes the test.

PRACTICAL EXAMPLE – QUESTIONMARK

Questionmark is a set of tools to help you design and delivery quizzes, examinations and tests. It is a widely used commercial product, available from http://www.questionmark. co.uk/uk/index.aspx.

Recognising and Recording Achievement (E1.1 Technology; E2.1 Technology)

The NIACE investigated possible ways of recognising and recording achievement (RARPA) through the use of technology (Clark and Hussain-Ahmed, 2006). This is known as paperless RARPA. RARPA is an approach designed for providers of non-accredited learning. It is based on five stages:

1. Determining the aims of the learner or a group of learners
2. Initial assessment
3. Agreeing learning objectives
4. Formative assessment
5. Summative and self-assessment.

The process has been used widely and successfully but it does tend to produce a large volume of paper records. Paperless RARPA aims to remove the need for paper records through the use of technology. Clark and Hussain-Ahmed (2006) identified a variety of ways of integrating technology into the RARPA process such as:

- Using an e-quiz to gain an initial impression of the learners' existing knowledge
- Capturing evidence through digital cameras, sound recording and video (especially useful in practical subjects such as dance)
- Self-assessment using a blog.

In many ways, the paperless RARPA approach transfers, in a straightforward and effective way, to any situation where you are seeking to provide a formative assessment.

Activity 6.4 Formative assessment

Consider your own subject and how you could recognise and record progress without using paper. What technologies would you consider to be the most appropriate? In particular, which approaches would lend themselves to maximum learner involvement?

Learners' needs in e-assessment (E2.1 Technology)

When changing to e-assessment, we often assume that learners will make the change from years of experience with conventional tests to using technology, both seamlessly and without any glitches. What we need to do is ensure that learners are familiar with the changes, have had a chance to practise using e-assessment and can perform to the best of their abilities. The Qualifications and Curriculum Authority guide (2007) to e-assessment states that we must ensure that learners are 'not disadvantaged by taking an on-screen test'.

Many awarding bodies provide practice materials and guidance for delivering e-assessment. These should be employed to help learners become confident in the tests before being faced with the summative assessment. It is very poor practice for learners to undertake an e-assessment without being familiar with it. Some basic issues that learners need to know are:

1. How to return to an answer
2. How to change an answer
3. What types of questions are they going to encounter (e.g. multiple choice, fill in spaces, enter text, etc.)
4. What they need to bring with them
5. What the assessment rules are (e.g. no mobile phones).

The digital skills of learners vary and many tests are based on being able to navigate through computer-based materials and manipulate objects displayed on the screen. E-tests often involve:

- Dragging and dropping objects
- Moving forwards and backwards through the material
- Selecting links
- Entering text into a designated area
- Selecting a check box to indicate an answer.

To ensure that learners are not placed at a disadvantage due to a lack of digital skills and confidence, they need the opportunity to practise the type of e-assessment and receive feedback and support to improve to the required standard.

Activity 6.5 Case studies

Efutures (www.efutures.org) is an online resource to help with the implementation of e-assessment. It contains a variety of case studies and you should visit the site to explore those case studies that are relevant to your needs.

Self-assessment (E3.1 Technology)

A key feature of learning is the ability of learners to assess their own work. Self-assessment involves the learners in considering:

- What they have achieved?
- How they can improve?

This often requires the learners to compare their performance against competency frameworks that define precisely what is needed, with learning objectives or outcomes. Technology can assist with self-assessment through a range of approaches including:

- E-portfolios
- Blogs
- Wikis.

E-portfolios

An e-portfolio is not simply a collection of evidence. It should to be dynamic with learners needing to review and assess their collection to identify what is the most appropriate evidence, mapping the evidence against assessment frameworks and reflecting on the material. Figure 6.2 showed five processes that are involved:

- Peer assessment
- Self-assessment
- Reflection
- Review
- Feedback.

The individual learners need to review their evidence regularly to identify if it is the most appropriate, what gaps there are and what further items are needed. This is often assisted by checklists, competency frameworks, comparisons with learning objectives and outcomes. These can be presented electronically and the results of self-assessments recorded for future use. E-portfolios also provide the opportunity for feedback on their self-assessment from peers and tutors, so that they can improve their skills.

A significant aspect of e-portfolios is the sharing of items with your peer group and tutors. This allows learners to see how other people have tackled tasks and their reflections of the experience. This provides comparisons for their own work and self-assessment. Without an understanding of the group standards, it can be difficult to self-assess on any reasonable basis.

Blogs

Blogs are focused on reflecting on learning experiences, which could be presented as assessing your performance in order to identify what you have achieved and what you now need to do to improve. Reflective blogging again has the advantages of feedback on your assessment of the experience from peers and tutors so that you can improve your skills. Many occupations now state that they require reflective practitioners who can learn from their experience. Blogging has the additional benefit of developing your reflective skills.

Wikis

Wikis allow a group to enter and edit each others' work so it is a mixture of peer and self-assessment. It allows the learners to see, in the context of a group project, how their work is received by others and how they judge their peers' contributions. The individuals can edit their own and their peers' work as well as experiencing the overall views of the group.

PRACTICAL EXAMPLE – ONLINE VOICE RECORDING

One way that learners can be encouraged to self-assess and reflect on their performance is through online voice recorders. Vocaroo is a website that provides a straightforward way of recording your voice, posting the results to a website or sending a speech e-mail. It is available at http://www.vocaroo.com/.

Feedback to learners (E4.1 Technology)

The feedback you provide to your learners can have many positive benefits such as:

- Helping them become more self-sufficient for their own learning
- Assisting them to learn from the errors they have made
- Reflecting on their work
- Gaining self-confidence and self-esteem.

Technology can assist you in giving feedback in a variety of different ways. Some examples are:

- Using a video of the learners' performances to help them see how they can improve manual skills (e.g. joining pipes, cutting hair, lifting heavy objects, sports activities and operating machines)
- Annotating assignments using comments and track changes so that the learners can see both their efforts and your comments
- Summarising an online discussion so that everyone can see where they have agreed and disagreed
- Comments on an entry in a learning diary or journal
- Comments on a discussion forum.

Feedback can be provided as a normal part of the course, either informally through your involvement in the learners' activities or more formally in individual reviews. The use of technology can apply to both and is only changed by your intentions and objectives. The giving of feedback should follow a well-known approach that applies to all feedback, whether using technology or not. It is:

- Start with positives showing the learners what they have done well

- Identify weaknesses and clearly show what the learners need to do to improve

- End on positives so the learners leave motivated to do better.

This approach can be applied to written feedback, group or individual comments, face-to-face reviews or online discussions.

Learners gain from feedback, and your relationship with them will improve as an outcome of giving feedback. Silence leaves learners in doubt and distances them from you.

Feedback from learners (E4.2 Technology)

There is a variety of technological ways of encouraging and obtaining feedback from learners. Earlier, we considered the use of voting technology and text walls. Both of these gain relatively immediate comments from a group of learners but in some cases you may want to gain more reflective thoughts that represent the whole group. One way to do this is to develop an online discussion group and encourage debate about the aspects that are most useful to you. This allows each individual to contribute and provides the overall group with individual comments to be taken into account. It can also help you focus discussion though asking additional questions or summarising learners' feedback.

Chapter 5 discussed researching learners' views and the methods employed there can be used as part of assessment feedback. These are:

- Online surveys

- Interviews (e.g. audio recorded)

- Focus groups (e.g. video recorded).

All these methods suggest that you are seeking feedback on a particular occasion while in practice it is often beneficial to gain the views of your learners throughout the course so that ideas and comments are not lost. The text wall approach can easily be adapted to be available throughout the course, creating a course notice board that grows during the programme.

No matter what means that you employ to obtain feedback, its value will depend on the relationship that you have with your learners. Good quality feedback will be gained if they trust you and believe that their feedback will be positively responded to. Without this relationship the feedback will probably be poor.

The final issue in gaining learner feedback is to act upon it so as to improve your assessment methods and approaches. It is a waste if you do not respond to feedback.

Quality standards (E5.1 Technology)

Assessment is the keystone of education and training. It is often governed by both your own organisation and external bodies' standards. There is a range of external organisations that set quality standards for assessment, such as awarding bodies, sector skills councils and funding agencies. These need to be followed otherwise the assessment may be invalid. It is important that you are aware of the quality standards that govern assessment in your organisation and subject.

Activity 6.6 Quality standards

Identify the quality standards controlling the qualification assessment that your learners undertake. Review the advice and guidance provided by your awarding body. What do you have to do and how does it impact on the use of technology? Often the awarding body's website offers helpful information and guidance (e.g. OCR (2010) 'Guide to Controlled Assessment' – this is an interactive document that contains guidance for teachers).

The quality standards will have an impact throughout your course. They will influence the content of the e-ILP and e-portfolios. Standards often specify factors that will influence the learners' studies, such as the nature of acceptable evidence (e.g. no evidence more than three years old). These standards will have a large impact on the learners and on their individual learning plan.

Activity 6.7 Quality assurance in the post-compulsory education sector

Using the Excellence Gateway portal, identify the features of the post-compulsory education quality assurance system and consider how it impacts on your teaching.

Chapter 5 includes discussion of the quality assurance of learning materials, online courses and other areas through approaches such as peer review.

Learners taking responsibility (E3.1 Technology)

E-learning is often based around the objective of developing learners to take responsibility for their own learning. This is a key characteristic that many employers look for in their employees. Several assessment approaches motivate learners to accept responsibility for their own learning and assessment, including:

- E-portfolios
- Learning journals
- Wikis
- Discussion groups.

E-portfolios are based around individuals identifying and collecting evidence that demonstrates that they are competent or have achieved specific learning outcomes. This places the responsibility on the learners themselves to succeed. The teacher's role is to support the learners in these tasks by providing feedback on the suitability of evidence and similar activities.

Learning journals are intended to encourage learners to reflect on their experiences, thereby helping them identify what are their strengths and weaknesses. Reflection assists with the process of deep learning through developing a complete understanding. Although you can help learners to reflect by demonstrating what they should consider (e.g. comparing experiences), it essentially requires that learners are motivated to undertake the task.

Wikis are about working as a team to agree jointly a document, a plan, a set of objectives or something similar. They are often used in assessment activities to provide a group context. The development of the wiki outcome is dependent on learners taking the initiative to contribute to the outcome by editing the existing content or adding new material. It is thus focused on individual responsibility, to contribute and agree with the other group members as to what is the way forward.

Discussion groups provide the means for everyone to contribute on an equal footing. The more extrovert members of the group cannot easily block the quieter participants. Anyone can post a message at any time so when contributions are assessed, it is a fairer comparison than a face-to-face discussion or project work. Responsibility for sending messages rests solely with the individual.

Technology is a means of developing personal responsibility and becoming an independent learner.

Summary

The main points of this chapter are:

- There has been a significant growth in e-assessment that employs technology to assess learners' progress and achievement. Technology is used to enhance both formative and summative assessment.

- E-portfolios are collections of digital evidence that show the learners' skills, knowledge and understanding. There are four types of e-portfolio – assessment, developmental, reflective and showcasing.

- An e-portfolio is a collection of evidence that is not a random pile of documents, recordings and other digital resources but is carefully selected to meet a distinct purpose.

- Formative assessment aims to help learners improve by providing feedback on their performance.

- Summative assessment is intended to be the final judgement on the learner's performance.

- Ownership of e-portfolio content is important. Learners must be free to transfer their portfolios' contents so that they can continue to use them after the end of the course.

- Many professions require members to become reflective practitioners since this leads to deep learning. A learning diary is one way of encouraging reflection.

- To create a test, you need to develop a question or task that, if successfully answered or completed, means that the learner has achieved the objective.

- Peer assessment is increasingly being used in group work and is assisted by the provision of specific criteria on which learners can judge their colleagues.

- Diagnostic tests are intended to help you identify the learning weaknesses individuals may have, so that you can design an appropriate programme for them.

- NIACE investigated how to assess non-accredited learning in order to recognise and record achievement. Their approach is called RARPA.

- Learners will often need support when using e-assessment methods.

- E-assessment often allows the learners to self-assess.

- Technology can assist you when giving feedback (e.g. by using video, annotating assignments, summarising an online discussion and commenting on learning diary entries).

- Technology can encourage learners to provide feedback to their teachers (e.g. voting technology, twitter and text walls).

- Assessment is a critical feature in education and training and is often controlled by external quality standards from awarding bodies, sector skills councils and funding agencies.

- E-learning is often based around the objective of developing learners who can take responsibility for their own learning. This is a key characteristic that many employers are seeking in their employees.

7

Access and Progression

Teaching standards (LLUK, 2007)

The standard statements FS1 to FS4 with the associated technology elements F1.1 to F4.1 Technology are covered in this chapter. It is concerned with using technology to help learners progress. Many parts of the earlier chapters will relate to this one, in particular Chapters 2 and 3.

Introduction

Education and training is not simply about helping a learner successfully study for a qualification or gain an understanding of a subject. It is also about helping learners develop self-confidence, self-esteem and a range of other generic skills. Often learners are on a journey of which your course is only a step along the way. They need to be assisted to make the right choices by being helped to be aware of the options available to them such as:

- The qualifications and grades required for entry into a profession or higher level course
- Career choices and their requirements
- What sources of help are available to them.

It is often difficult to judge the teacher's role in many of these areas. At a minimum you have a role in signposting services and information sources so that learners are aware of assistance available to them. Advice and information are valued by learners.

Communication technology has the potential to provide learners with access to information about almost any topic. The Oxford Internet survey (Dutton and

Helsper, 2007) showed that the Internet was rapidly becoming the first choice for informal learning. In 2007, 84 per cent of students used the Internet as their first choice for finding information. By 2009, this had risen to 100 per cent (Dutton, Helsper and Gerber, 2009). It is obvious that online sources are probably the most useful to offer your learners.

Learners' journey

The learning journey that is defined in the DFES's Skills for Life strategy (Excellence Gateway, n.d.) identifies a series of steps for learners to follow to improve their literacy and numeracy. These steps are also relevant for the study of any subject. They are:

1. Signposting – information, advice and guidance (IAG) to identify the appropriate learning path for individual learners to help them realise their goals

2. Initial assessment – to help the learner select the appropriate learning course or programme

3. Diagnostic assessment – to assess the learner's characteristics

4. Individual learning plan – steps 2 and 3 can make important contributions to the plan

5. Learning experiences – this is obviously a key part of the teacher's direct responsibility and also where e-learning can make a large contribution

6. Formative assessment – regular feedback to help the learners identify strengths and weaknesses in order to improve their performance

7. Summative assessment – final assessment to achieve the course objective (e.g. qualification).

The steps essentially form a cycle through which the learners travel until they reach their objective. The teacher's role could perhaps be described as assisting them to navigate the path. In the earlier chapters of this book, the benefits that e-learning can bring to the various steps have been discussed. Chapter 6 covered the assessment steps, Chapters 3 and 4 step 5, with Chapter 5 assisting in the planning and design of the whole process.

The learning journey has been described in other ways. For many learners, it is a lifelong process and a single cycle is simply the beginning of the process. Plans and objectives will change as life and careers alter or are challenged. Learning is part of these developments and technology can play a critical role in helping people to cope with change.

Lifelong e-portfolios (F2.1 Technology)

In earlier sections of this book we have considered the use of e-portfolios for a variety of purposes. One role is to provide a lifelong record of achievement and experience, a store that can be used no matter what changes in our lives. It can offer a foundation on which to build, assist the learners move from education to work and work to education as it becomes necessary. It supports the lifelong learning journey that can have many different transitions such as:

- further to higher education
- adult and community learning to work
- work to training.

Each experience can be recorded in the learner's e-portfolio, enabling the individual to have a complete record that will support any changes that they need or desire to make. This is often expressed in the example of producing customised CV to meet the needs of the job for which they are applying. In addition, the records can also help with gaining entry to education programmes that may offer a non-qualifications route to those who can demonstrate the relevant experience. The teacher's role is to motivate the learners in the long-term task of developing and maintaining their e-portfolio by convincing them of the benefits that it can bring to them.

A lifelong learning e-portfolio will become very large if maintained over decades and so needs to be designed with care to ensure that the required resources can be easily located. This requires an effective folder structure, a good search engine and a consistent use of tags. The long-term storage of information will be aided by a regular and systematic review of the evidence to ensure that the most appropriate is held.

We have so far considered the use of a portfolio to support the learners once they have decided where they want to go, but it can also be useful to help individuals come to decisions, often through the power of reflection. A learning journal will often form part of an e-portfolio. Reflection not only allows learners to achieve deep learning but also to consider their experiences and arrive at conclusions about their own progression. Again, the teacher's role is to encourage and explain the benefits of reflection to the learner. This may well come from using a journal for specific course objectives, so demonstrating its potential. The key is not simply to focus on the short term but to consider the long-term applications.

Learners' opportunities and choices (F1.1 Technology; F2.1 Technology)

Most colleges and other providers offer more than education and training. They offer assistance to progress learners' studies by providing information about the choices available both within the institution and with other providers. This is not simply about education and training options but often covers job opportunities, financial support and specialist help.

Katsifli (2010), in a review of evidence about the use of VLEs and particularly the blackboard system, identified significant use in relation to supporting learners to access information. VLEs can be used for many information purposes such as:

- Administration of their courses
- Distributing course documents (e.g. study guides, assignments and results)
- Keeping learners up to date with developments
- College developments (e.g. announcements).

VLEs are also useful in providing learners with access to information about help and assistance such as:

- Organisations that can offer learners assistance
- Choices of progression routes
- Job finding.

Your role has a teacher is often simply to make learners aware that these sources of information are available. You do have the extra potential to make available your specialist knowledge and experience by providing information on the VLE, participating in discussion forums or making opportunities available to your learners that become known to you through your own networks.

What do employers want?

Many learners are undertaking courses in order to improve their prospects of employment. Employers are not simply seeking particular qualifications but also generic skills, abilities and the right attitude. In addition, getting a job or obtaining a place on a course is not simple because it also requires the ability to complete an application form, write a letter and answer questions in an interview. Learners need to know effective ways to do these. The trend in Great Britain is for the number of unskilled jobs to reduce and the number of skilled ones to increase. This is compounded by the pace of change, making it inevitable that employees will need to retrain several times during their lives. Every learner needs not only to be able to understand how to find and apply for jobs but also to progress in education and training.

Activity 7.1 What do employers want from their employees?

Employers require a variety of skills and abilities from their employees. These are not limited to the skills relating to a particular occupation but include other skills such as team working. Use the Internet to search for the skills, knowledge and abilities employers want and produce a list to consider against your course. What could you do to help your learners develop the required skills and abilities?

Activity 7.2 Online resources for progression

The Excellence Gateway has downloadable resources to help teachers encourage and assist their learners to progress. Explore the resources available at http://tlp.excellencegateway.org.uk/tlp/progression/aboutprogress/index.html and identify what would be most appropriate for your learners.

How technology can support learners' progress

Technology can assist access to learning and progress in a variety of ways. Some examples are:

- Using the wealth of online resources – there are many websites that offer advice, information and guidance to individuals to help them gather the information they need to make decisions about their careers. The links to them can be gathered together in order that the learners' previous experiences can be made available to future ones. Delicious (http://delicious.com/) is a social bookmarking tool with which you can create lists of bookmarks of websites that are linked to access and progression. These links can be shared with other users enabling you to see the resources that other people who are interested in the same topics have saved.

- Employment assistance is offered by a range of sites, including national newspapers such as *The Guardian* (http://tlp.excellencegateway.org.uk/tlp/progression/aboutprogress/index.html). You can register with these sites, giving them key features of the jobs you are seeking and they will automatically match you to vacancies. You are notified of the matches by e-mail. Some sites allow you to enter your CV details so that you can be promoted to employers. There is also advice on finding a job and a variety of other facilities.

- Social networking – Linkedin is a social network aimed at professionals who want to network with others, gaining the benefits of contacts in many fields and also the opportunity to advertise their own skills and experience. It allows users to present their experience, qualifications and knowledge and is available at http://www.linkedin.com/.

- Recruitment agencies offer online facilities whereby job seekers register with them to gain access to vacancies and employers. In addition, many employers now advertise their vacancies online making it important for learners to have the skills and understanding to use these facilities effectively.

- Office applications can be used to help learners organise their job- and course-seeking activities. It is a time consuming task to complete applications, covering letters and CVs. However, by using applications such as word processing, the learners can save time by reusing their earlier efforts. This needs to be done with care, however, since each application must be customised to meet the employer's requirements.

Technology has a huge potential to help learners, but it can also have some risks. Posting information and photographs on social networking sites is naive if you believe that only friends will see them. Many employers and educational providers now routinely search the Internet for information about candidates. They will not be impressed by photographs showing bad behaviour. Learners must be aware that anything they post online is potentially in the public domain and available to everyone.

PRACTICAL EXAMPLE – FAST TOMATO

Fast Tomato is an online interactive resource for learners over 12 years old who are seeking careers advice and guidance. It is widely used in many schools and colleges and is available at http://www.fasttomato.com/index.aspx.

Learning providers' websites

Many colleges and other education and training providers use their websites and other online services to present prospective learners with a view of what studying with them will be like. This is quite important as there is a growing trend to base decisions on online sources in preference to other information. The information about the course must be accurate to avoid misleading learners and thus losing potentially suitable candidates simply because of misunderstandings through poor presentation of information.

Some straightforward ways of improving website design are:

■ Easy website navigation – a simple straightforward structure in which users cannot get lost

■ Consistent presentation so users can easily learn where to look for particular types of information

■ Short webpages so that users do not have to scroll down long pages with the risk of getting confused and lost

■ Clear and concise presentation of information.

It is critical that the website conforms to accessibility standards. Techdis offer advice to designers and others involved in websites helping them make their sites accessible to all learners.

Activity 7.3 How others see us

Visit your own organisation's website and try to locate information about the course you teach. What was the experience like? Could you locate accurate information about the course? How easy was it to use the website to find information?

Activity 7.4 Accessibility standards

W3C is a worldwide consortium that develops guidelines for designers and others to produce accessible websites. Undertake a search of the World Wide Web and learn about their guidelines. Many people believe that by following these, they produce websites that are easier to use by all people and not just disabled users. Consider the guidelines and see whether you agree that they would assist everyone.

Some education and training institutions go beyond the simple presentation of information, helping potential learners decide whether they are the right place for them to study and offering pre-course material so that learners start studying before the course starts formally.

Activity 7.5 Pre-course learning activities

Consider your own course. What pre-course learning activities and information would you provide for learners? You may wish to reflect on the purpose of pre-course work and its effects (e.g. if only a minority of of learners undertake it). What is the aim of the activities?

Another possibility is to offer post-course activities and information to aid learners who have completed the course.

Activity 7.6 Post-course learning activities

Consider your own course. What post-course learning activities and information would you provide for learners? You may wish to reflect on the purpose of post-course work and its effects. What is the aim of the activities?

Supporting learning (F2.1 Technology)

Throughout this book we have discussed many uses of technology to support learners. Table 7.1 summarises some of the ways that these tools could be used to help learners to progress.

Developing learners' confidence and self-esteem through technology

A key role in access and progression for all teachers is to help learners develop their self-confidence and self-esteem. Without confidence in themselves and their abilities,

TABLE 7.1 E-learning tools and progression

TOOLS AND APPROACHES	NOTES
Social networking	This is a means of allowing peer support and networks of learners to form so as to assist each other.
Discussion groups	Discussion groups with a focus on learners' next steps could have the potential to encourage collaboration and mutual support. In addition, they could be encouraged to discuss relevant topics such as interview techniques and to share experiences and information.
VLEs	VLEs offer a way of presenting sources of information and links to relevant websites so that learners can access them at their convenience.
Podcasts	Podcasts covering appropriate progression topics can easily be created so that learners can listen to them in a flexible way.
E-assessment	Assessment can often help learners decide on their next steps.
Text messages	These are a quick and effective means of making announcements, reminding learners of events and allowing them to network with each other from almost anywhere.
Wikis	Wikis provide a collaborative environment in which groups of learners can work together to create useful outcomes, such as developing a letter of application or the perfect CV.
Blogs	Blogs allow learners to develop reflective skills by reviewing their experiences. This can help prepare learners for interviews or assist with application letters and forms.
E-portfolios	A means of organising personal information and achievements to support job applications or further study.
Feedback	Many e-learning approaches provide the opportunity for feedback to the learner which can assist in consideration of their options.
Repositories	Learning content often provides materials aimed at assisting learners to develop relevant skills, for example, study skills.
Webquest	Groups of learners can compare and contrast different sources of access and progression information to decide what is the most useful to them.

learners will have low aspirations. Technology has been linked to developing self-confidence and esteem in adults who have had poor initial educational experiences. It is important to remember that each learner will have different needs, so young people may well need a different approach than do adults learning in community settings. Their aspirations may be very different. Learners will need access to appropriate IAG to make them aware of the possible routes, opportunities and careers open to them. IAG requires specialists, so do ask for assistance and, in particular, if you have learners with special needs (e.g. disabled learners).

Activity 7.7 Supporting different groups

Consider the various groups of learners that you teach. How would you use technology to support them in considering their future plans for progressing their learning and employment? You may like to consider:

1. Disabled learners
2. Adults returning to learning after a long break
3. Ex-offenders
4. Young people.

Professional knowledge (F3.1 Technology)

In Chapter 4 we discussed the application of technology to maintain and extend your professional skills and knowledge. The same methods can clearly be used to help you access professional knowledge that will assist your learners' progress. The main methods were:

- Searching the World Wide Web
- Using specialist search engines
- Employing Google alerts to make you aware of new developments
- Joining sector portals such as the Excellence Gateway
- Registering for appropriate online journals and e-newsletters
- Joining specialist discussion groups.

Activity 7.8 Gold Dust

Gold Dust (http://golddust.bdplearning.com/index.php), available through the LSIS, http://golddust.bdplearning.com/, provides resources and materials to help with teacher staff development. These include content to assist with access and progression. Visit the website and identify resources that would help your professional knowledge in order to assist your learners.

Specialist help (F4.1 Technology)

The help that learners need to enable them make decisions about careers, education and employment is often specialised and your role is probably limited to providing information about where to access the right services. Many specialist sources of help are now available online or they can be contacted through communication technologies. Providing information will probably require that you use communication technologies to contact colleagues and gain their help in identifying the right specialist services to suggest.

PRACTICAL EXAMPLE – JOBSEARCH PLUS

Jobsearch Plus maintains a database of vacancies that anyone can search online. It is straightforward to use and in some cases you can apply directly to the employer without contacting the Jobcentre Plus. It is available at http://www.direct.gov. uk/en/Employment/Jobseekers/LookingForWork/DG_10030134.

PRACTICAL EXAMPLE – CAREERS ADVICE FOR ADULTS

Careers advice and information for adults can be accessed online at http://careersadvice.direct.gov.uk/. The website offers a range of services and links including speaking to an adviser and joining a discussion forum.

A useful approach is to integrate into the course activities that involve locating or assessing online sources of specialist help.

Activity 7.9 Specialist services

Design a webquest that could be used by your learners to access for themselves the services offered by a range of advice and guidance agencies.

Summary

The main points of this chapter are:

- Learners' education and training journeys are not merely about obtaining qualifications but are also concerned with developing self-confidence, self-esteem and a range of other generic skills.
- The Oxford Internet survey (Dutton, Helsper and Gerber, 2009) showed that the Internet was rapidly becoming the first choice for finding information.
- E-portfolios can provide a lifelong record of achievement and experience to enable learners move from education to work and work to education, as it becomes necessary.

- One of the teacher's roles is to signpost available sources of information.
- The number of unskilled jobs is continuously reducing and the number of skilled ones is increasing alongside the rapid changes in the nature of work. This makes it inevitable that employees will need to retrain several times during their lives.
- Technology can assist access to learning and progress in many ways.
- There are risks as well as benefits for learners in using technology (e.g. posting information and photographs on social networking sites will often make them available to everyone, including employers and educational providers).
- Education and training providers often use their websites as the main way of presenting information about their courses, offering pre-course material for learners and post-course assistance in some cases.
- It is important to remember that each learner will have distinct needs, so different approaches will be needed for different groups.
- Many specialist sources of help are now available online or can be contacted through communication technologies.

Glossary

ALT – Association for Learning Technology

app – a shortened version of the term 'application'

asynchronous – communication methods where the sender and receiver do not have to be present at the same time (e.g. e-mail)

authoring – the process of creating of e-learning content

Becta – the British Education and Communication Technology Agency is currently the Government's agency for developing and promoting the use of technology in schools and, in some areas, the post-compulsory education sector. They are due to close in 2010/2011. The website will close on 31 January 2011 but will be captured on the National Archives (http://nationalarchives.gov.uk/)

blended learning – the integration of technology-enhanced learning with traditional methods to gain the best combination

blog – a website in which the content is presented in date order. It is often used to present individual views on issues while other users with access to the site can offer additional comments. It can be used as a learning diary in education and training

cloud – storing resources online so that you can access them from any location that has Internet access

computer-based learning – the term used in the early development of e-learning to describe the use of computer technology in education and training

CPD – continuous professional development

Creative Commons – a type of copyright licence that allows the owner to give freedom to users

CV – curriculum vitae

DDA – Disability and Discrimination Act

e-assessment – assessment that employs technology to deliver tests

e-ILP – Electronic individual learning plan

e-learning – a broad term intended to encompass all uses of electronic tools and systems that assist learning

e-portfolio – an organised collection of evidence that is intended for assessment, professional development, reflection or showcasing skills

ESOL – English for speakers of other languages

formative assessment – feedback to help develop a learner's understanding

GPS – global positioning system

IAG – information, advice and guidance

ICT – information and communication technology

information and learning technology (ILT) – an alternative term for e-learning, used in parts of the post-compulsory education sector

iPhone – an Internet-enabled mobile phone

IWB – the abbreviation sometimes used for interactive whiteboard

JISC – the Joint Information and Systems Committee is a higher education agency that supports the use of technology in education in UK universities and colleges

learning management system (LMS) – an alternative name for a VLE

LExDis – Disabled Learners' Experiences of E-Learning (project)

LLUK – Lifelong Learning United Kingdom

LSIS – Learning and Skills Improvement Service

lurking – taking part in a discussion group by reading messages but rarely posting your thoughts

m-learning – an abbreviation for mobile learning (e.g. using portable devices to learn)

MOMO – Mobile Moodle

NIACE – National Institute for Adult Continuing Education

online learning – learning through and with online communication methods (e.g. discussion forums)

PDA – a personal digital assistant, which is a mobile device offering access to the Internet and telephone facilities

PLE – a personal learning environment

podcast – an audio file that can be distributed using RSS or downloaded from a website. It is often used in education to provide learning material that the student can listen to while travelling

RARPA – recognising and recording achievement

RSS – Really Simple Syndication, an automatic distribution system that allows content to be sent to subscribers

SENDA – Special Educational Needs and Disability Act

Skype – see VoIP

synchronous – communication methods when the sender and receiver are present at the same time (e.g. telephone)

tag – a label given to content to classify it (e.g. reflection) so that it can be identified by search tools

technology-enhanced learning – the term used for the application of technology to enhance learning

VLE – virtual learning environment

VoIP – this stands for Voice over Internet Protocol and is better known as Skype. It is the means of sending speech over the Internet so you can hold a conversation with another user of the system

webquest – an enquiry-based online learning activity

wiki – a system in which a group of users can work together, entering and editing their input to create a joint document. Wikis are often used in education for group projects to encourage the development of team working

Resources

Accessibility – Techdis provides advice on the use of technology to assist disabled learners – www.techdis.org.uk

ALT – a membership website with resources for professional development and accreditation – http://www.alt.ac.uk/

BBC – the television company offers a range online materials covering many subjects for both adults and children (e.g. Webwise – basic ICT), literacy and learning English. It is available from http://www.bbc.co.uk/learning/

Becta – government national agency for e-learning – http://www.becta.org.uk

Books – specialist search engines to locate new, second hand and out-of-print books: Google Books – http://books.google.co.uk/; Abebooks – second-hand books – http://www.abebooks.com/; Bookfinder – http://www.bookfinder.com/; BibliOZ – out of print books – http://www.biblioz.com/ and AddALL – http://www.addall.com/

British Education Index (BEI) – research database – http://www.leeds.ac.uk/bei/COLN/COLN_default.html

Campaign for Learning – promoting learning – http://www.campaign-for-learning.org.uk/cfl/index.asp

Careers Advice for Adults – the website for the adult careers service. It is available at http://careersadvice.direct.gov.uk/

E-books – a collection of e-books especially chosen for further education and available to colleges – http://fe.jiscebooksproject.org/

eFutures – a resource to support the use of e-assessment – http://e-assessment.org.uk/

Emerging Technologies – one of Becta's roles is to consider the potential of new technology developments in education – http://emergingtechnologies.becta.org.uk/

Excellence Gateway – resources for post-compulsory education – http://excellencegateway.org.uk

Futurelab – innovative use of technology in learning – http://www.futurelab.org.uk/

Google Books – online access to millions of books (see Books)

Infokits – a digital repository information key. It is available at http://www.jiscinfonet.ac.uk/infokits/repositories

Institute for Learning – the professional body for teachers in the post-compulsory sector – http://www.ifl.ac.uk/

JISC – supports research and development e-learning projects relating to higher education – http://www.jisc.ac.uk/

JISC Collections – access to an enormous set of digital education content – http://www.jisc-collections.ac.uk/

JISC Legal – advice on the legal implications of using technology in education – http://www.jisclegal.ac.uk/

JorumOpen – this is a repository of open educational resources that have been provided by higher and further education institutions. They are all free to use under a Creative Commons licence – http://open.jorum.ac.uk/xmlui/

LSIS – an agency that supports the post-compulsory education sector and is the manager of the Excellence Gateway

National Research and Development Centre for Adult Literacy and Numeracy – http://www.nrdc.org.uk/index.asp

NIACE – independent organisation supporting adult learning – http://www.niace.org.uk

NLN – access to a large collection of interactive chunks of learning material for use in the post-compulsory education sector – http://www.nln.ac.uk/

Ofqual – this is the regulatory authority for qualification – http://www.ofqual.gov.uk/

Ofsted Good Practice Database – http://www.excellencegateway.org.uk/page.aspx?o=goodpracticedatabase

OpenLearn – a large collection of Open University learning materials that is free to use – http://openlearn.open.ac.uk/

Plagiarism Advice Service – http://www.jiscpas.ac.uk/index.php

Staff Development Learning Centre (SDELC) – this provides learning materials and courses for teachers who are seeking to improve their e-learning skills. It is a free service that was developed by NIACE and is available at http://www.sdelc.co.uk/

Webquests – examples of webquests – http://questgarden.com/

Whiteboards – a website provided by the University of Cambridge that contains professional development materials for secondary school teachers in the form of video case studies on how to use electronic whiteboards, data projectors and other technology. The site is at http://t-media.educ.cam.ac.uk/

Tools

Audacity – a sound recording and editing application. It is widely used to create podcasts and is available from http://audacity.sourceforge.net/

Blogger – an online system that allows you to create blogs. It can be accessed at https://www.blogger.com/start. You will need to open a Google account but this is straightforward and free task

BrowseAloud – a tool that enables text presented on a webpage or in an acrobat (pdf) file to be read out aloud. It is available from http://www.browsealoud.com/

Crossword Creator – a tool that allows you to produce crosswords for assessment or revision. It is available at http://www.supercrosswordcreator.com/

Delicious – a social bookmarking tool that lets you create lists of bookmarks of websites that are linked to a particular theme. These lists can be shared with other users, enabling you to see resources that other people interested in the same topics have saved. It is available at http://delicious.com/

Dictionary – Dictionary.com is a free online dictionary. It is available at http://dictionary.reference.com/

DimDim – an online conferencing system that allows you to host small meetings for free, without the need to install any software. It is available from http://www.dimdim.com/

Edmodo –a free online virtual classroom. It is available at http://www.edmodo.com/

Edu Apps – collections of useful applications for education and training and available from http://www.rsc-ne-scotland.ac.uk/eduapps/

Elgg – a social network creation tool, available at http://elgg.org/

Elluminate – a commercial virtual classroom used widely in education. It is available from http://www.elluminate.com/

e-portfolios – there are a wide range of portfolios available. Some are open source, such as Mahara, (http://mahara.org/), while others are commercial products such as Pebblepad (http://www.pebblepad.co.uk/)

eXe, the eLearning XHTML editor – an open source authoring tool that will help you create learning materials. It is available from http://exelearning.org/

Fast Tomato – an online interactive resource for learners over 12 years old who are seeking careers advice and guidance. It is available at http://www.fasttomato.com/index.aspx

FreeMind – a mind mapping application, available at http://freemind.sourceforge.net/wiki/index.php/Main_Page

Google Alerts – a way of keeping up to date with developments associated with a particular subject. It is available at http://www.google.com/alerts?hl=en&gl=

Google Calendar – an online calendar that can be shared with others, letting you create group schedules or individual ones. It is available through Google Docs

Google Docs – a set of online applications that are free to use once you have registered for a Google mail account. It provides a word-processor, spreadsheet, form designer, folders to store files online and a presentation application. They are available through Google search engine

Google Reader – an online aggregator that can read RSS feeds. It is available through the Google search engine

Groupsite – a social networking tool that allows you to create networks. It is available at http://www.groupsite.com/

Hot Potatoes – Hot Potatoes is a group of applications that are aimed at creating educational materials for different types of assessment, including self-assessment. The applications are freeware and are available from http://hotpot.uvic.ca/

iGoogle – a service that allows you to create an individualised webpage that links you to all the sites and online services you employ. It is available through the Google search engine

Jing – a screen capture and video tool. It is available from http://www.jingproject.com/

Jobsearch Plus – an online database of vacancies that anyone can search. It is available at http://www.direct.gov.uk/en/Employment/Jobseekers/LookingForWork/DG_10030134

Linkedin – a social network aimed at professionals, available at http://www.linkedin.com/

Mahara – an open source e-portfolio system. It is available from http://mahara.org

Mindmeister – a collaborative online mind mapping tool. It is available from http://www.mindmeister.com/

Mindomo – an online mind mapping tool, available from http://www.mindomo.com/

Ning – a private social networking tool. It is available from http://www.ning.com/

PBwiki+ – this is now called PBworks

PBworks – a wiki creation tool. It is available at http://pbworks.com/content/edu+overview

Pebblepad – an e-portfolio system, available from http://www.pebblepad.co.uk/

Photostory 3.0 for Windows – this tool helps you create learning materials based around a still image with a voice narrative. It is a free application from Microsoft and available from http://www.microsoft.com/windowsxp/using/digitalphotography/PhotoStory/default.mspx

Polldaddy – an online survey creation resource. It is available at http://polldaddy.com/

Polleverywhere – an online tool that allows you to undertake polls using text messaging. It is available from http://www.polleverywhere.com/

Prezi – an online presentation tool, available at http://prezi.com/

Quandary – a tool for developing interactive case studies. It is available from http://www.halfbakedsoftware.com/quandary.php

Snippy – a tool for capturing screens. It is available at http://www.bhelpuri.net/Snippy/

SocialGo – a tool that enables you to create social networks them. It is available from http://www.socialgo.com/

Spruz – a social network creation tool, available at http://www.spruz.com/

Survey Monkey – an online survey system that allows you to create and undertake surveys. It is available from http://www.surveymonkey.com/

TodaysMeet – an online collaborative space that helps collaborative working. It is available at http://www.todaysmeet.com/

Turnitin – an online plagiarism checker. It is available at http://turnitin.com/static/index.html

Virtual Training Suite – this is an online collection of tutorials covering a range of subjects but aimed at helping you develop searching skills in the context of higher education. It is available at http://www.vts.intute.ac.uk/

Vocaroo – an online voice recorder. It is available at http://www.vocaroo.com/

VoiceThread – a website that allows users to share and discuss content (e.g. documents). It is available at http://voicethread.com/#home

Wallwisher – this is an online facility that lets you create an online notice board where users can add notes. This is often used to gain feedback from a group – http://www.wallwisher.com

Wink – a tool for creating learning materials through screen captures and thus mostly aimed at learning about software and applications. It is available at http://www.debugmode.com/wink/

Wordle – an online tool that creates a word cloud from a document based on the frequency that words appear in the text. It is available at http://www.wordle.net/

WordPress – a tool for creating blogs, available at http://wordpress.org/

Xerte – a tool to help you create interactive browser-based learning materials. It is available from http://www.nottingham.ac.uk/xerte/toolkits.htm

XMind – a mind mapping application, available from http://www.xmind.net/

References

Becta (2009), *Safeguarding Learners in the Digital World*, accessed on 15 February 2011, www.becta.org.uk.

Becta (2010), *Harnessing Technology Review 2009: The Role of Technology in Further Education and Skills*, accessed on 22 April 2010, http://feandskills.becta.org.uk/display.cfm?resID=41523&page=1886&catID=1868.

Bennett, L. and Reynolds, C. (2009), 'Is Podcasting an Effective Component of Online Learning', in The Post-Conference Reflections of Learning from Learners' Experience Conference, University of Greenwich.

Betts, S. and Kambouri, M. (2007), *Using Voting Technology for Assessment*, London: National Research and Development Centre for Adult Literacy and Numeracy.

Bloom, B.S. (1956), *Taxonomy of Educational Objectives: The classification of Educational Goals*, New York: David McKay.

Cercone, K. (2008), 'Characteristics of Adult Learners with Implications for Online Learning Design', *AACE Journal*, 16 (2), 137–159.

Clark, A. and Hussain-Ahmed, S. (2006), *Signalling Success, Paper-free Approaches to Recognising and Recording Learner Progress and Achievement*, Leicester: NIACE.

Clark, R.C. and Mayer, R.E. (2003), *E-learning and the Science of Instruction*, San Francisco: Pfeiffer.

Clarke, A. (2001a), *Assessing the Quality of Open and Distance Learning Materials*, Leicester: NIACE.

Clarke, A. (2001b), *Designing Computer-Based Learning Materials*, Basingstoke: Gower.

Clarke, A. (2003), *ICT a New Basic Skill*, Leicester: NIACE.

Clarke, A. (2008), *E-learning Skills*, Second Edition, Basingstoke: Palgrave Macmillan.

Close, A., Hesse, C. and De Cicco, E. (2009), *Online Learning Matters*, Leicester: NIACE.

Cochrane, T.D. (2010), 'Exploring Mobile Learning Success Factors', *Association of Learning Technology Journal*, 18 (2), 133–148.

Cox, M., Webb, M., Abbott, C., Blakeley, B., Beauchamp, T. and Rhodes, V. (2003), *ICT and Pedagogy: A Review of the Research Literature*, ICT in Schools Research and Evaluation Series no. 18, London: Department for Education and Skills.

Davis Dyslexia Association International (2010), 'Website Design of Dyslexia Users', accessed on 29 July 2010, http://www.dyslexia.com/library/webdesign.htm.

Department for Education and Skills (2001), *Skills for Life: The National Strategy for Improving Adult Literacy and Numeracy Skills*, London: Department for Education and Skills.

Dodge, B. (2010), 'Webquest', accessed on 2 August 2010, http://questgarden.com/.

Dutton, W.H. and Helsper, E.J. (2007), *The Internet in Britain*, Oxford: Oxford Internet Institute, University of Oxford.

Dutton, W.H., Helsper, E.J. and Gerber, M.M. (2009), *The Internet in Britain*, Oxford: Oxford Internet Institute, University of Oxford.

Excellence Gateway (n.d.), 'Learning Journey Diagram', accessed on 25 August 2010, http://www.excellence-gateway.org.uk/page.aspx?o=158509.

Futurelab (2010), 'Digital Literacy across the Curriculum', accessed on 14 May 2010, www.futurelab.org.uk/projects/digital-participation.

Gosper, M., Green, D., McNeill, M., Phillips, R., Preston, G. and Woo, K. (2008), *The Impact of Web-based Lecture Technologies on Current and Future Practices in Learning and Teaching*, Sydney: Australian Learning and Teaching Council.

Hartley, P. (1998), *Learning and Studying: A Research Perspective*, London: Routledge.

JISC (2007), 'In Their Own Words: Exploring the Learner's Perspective on E-learning', accessed on 26 March 2010, www.jisc.ac.uk.

JISC (2008), 'Effective Practice with e-Portfolios: Supporting 21st Century Learning', accessed on 26 March 2010, www.jisc.ac.uk.

JISC (2009a), 'Effective Practice in a Digital Age: A Guide to Technology-enhanced Learning and Teaching', accessed on 26 March 2010, www.jisc.ac.uk.

JISC (2009b), 'Responding to Learners: A Guide to Embedding the Learner's Voice', accessed on 26 March 2010, www.jisc.ac.uk/.

Katsifli, D. (2010), *The Impact of Blackboard Software on Education Globally over the Past Ten Years*, Amsterdam: Blackboard International.

Kolb, D.A. (1984), *Experiential Learning Experience as a Source of Learning and Development*, Englewood Cliffs, NJ: Prentice Hall.

Lexdis (2010), http://www.lexdis.org.uk/, accessed on 26 March 2010.

LLUK (2007), 'New Overarching Professional Standards for Teachers, Tutors and Trainers in the Lifelong Learning Sector', accessed on 14 March 2010, http://www.lluk.org/documents/professional_standards_for_itts_020107.pdf.

LSIS (2010), LSIS Policy Update 6, 7 to 21 July 2010, Coventry: LSIS.

McNaught, C. (2001), 'Quality Assurance for Online Courses: From Policy to Process to Improvement?', Ascilite Conference, accessed on 20 August 2010, http://www.ascilite.org.au/conferences/melbourne01/pdf/papers/mcnaughtc.pdf.

Mason, R. and Rennie, F. (2010), 'Web-based course design, ALT-Wiki', accessed on 30 June 2010, http://wiki.alt.ac.uk/index.php/Web-based_course_design.

Mayes, T. (2006), 'LEX Methodology Report', accessed on 3 August 2010, http://www.jisc.ac.uk/media/documents/programmes/elearningpedagogy/lex_method_final.pdf.

OCR (2010), 'Guide to Controlled Assessment: Speaking GCSE French, German and Spanish', Volume 3, May 2010, accessed on 23 August 2010, http://www.ocr.org.uk/download/sm/ocr_30076_sm_gcse_ca_guide.pdf.

Ofcom (2009), 'Managing your Media: a Consumer Guide to Protecting your Children in a Digital World', accessed on 15 February 2011, www.ofcom.org.uk.

Office of Public Sector Information (n.d.), 'The Special Educational Needs and Disability Act 2001', accessed on 20 August 2010, http://www.legislation.gov.uk/.

Ofqual (2010a), 'Maintaining Standards in On-demand Testing using Item Response Theory', accessed on 22 March 2010, http://www.ofqual.gov.uk/.

Ofqual (2010b), 'Regulatory Research into On-demand Testing', accessed on 22 March 2010, http://www.ofqual.gov.uk/.

Qualifications and Curriculum Authority (2007), 'E-assessment: Guide to Effective Practice', accessed on 11 May 2010, www.efutures.org.

Salmons, G. (2004), *E-moderating: The Key to Teaching and Learning Online*, Second Edition, London: Routledge.

Schuller, T. and Watson, D. (2009), *Learning Through Life: Inquiry into the Future for Lifelong Learning*, Leicester: NIACE.

Sharples, M., Graber, R., Harrison, C. and Logan, K. (2008), *E-safety and Web 2.0: Web 2.0 Technologies for Learning at Key Stages 3 and 4*. Coventry: Becta.

Tait, M. (n.d.), 'Will the Role of the Teacher Change with the Use of ICT, Campaign for Learning', accessed on 19 August 2010, http://www.campaign-for-learning.org.uk/cfl/learninginschools/projects/learning-tolearn/learning_to_learn_in_fe_project.asp.

Techdis (2007), 'Accessibility Essentials 3: Creating Accessibility Presentations', accessed on 20 August 2010, http://www.techdis.ac.uk/.

Thomson (2005), 'Drivers and barriers to the adoption of e-Assessment for UK Awarding Bodies', accessed on 22 March 2010, http://www.ofqual.gov.uk/.

Index